Stepping Stones
In the beginning was the Word.

Ken Harvey

OWL
PUBLISHING

Owl Publishing, LLC.
Ephrata, Pennsylvania

www.owlpublishinghouse.com

ISBN: 978-1-949929-79-9

Dedication

This book is dedicated to my mom who recently passed away. I didn't know how to say I love you back but hope that you are proud of me from heaven.

Contents

Acknowledgments

I would like to acknowledge all the people in my life that made my journey to the pros possible. While God is the key, there were so many people he used along the way. I may not have mentioned you by names or have left out a lot of chapters in my life, but you all know who you are. I am forever grateful. This book is also for the dreamers, the believers, the ones who may have lost faith. Like a football game, this is only my first half. There is a lot more to the story, but that's the second quarter.

Prologue

The Watkins Award recognizes the contributions of four outstanding African American student-athletes, and I was asked to emcee the event. These outstanding young men were discovered from a nationwide search by the National Alliance of African American Athletics selections committee. Because I didn't do well in high school, my chances of receiving this honor were slim to none, but I had previously emceed and was grateful when they invited me back. Thank God for the power of being a celebrity. The glitzy conference room in downtown Washington D.C. was the ideal venue for this event, which was always well attended by past alumni, family, and friends of the award winners. I scanned the room, admiring well-dressed men and women. The love that enveloped the room created a warm and welcoming feeling of the wealth that comes from family and mutual admiration. I stumbled a bit on my lines but manage to keep the program going at a steady pace, which was my assignment for the evening.

When it was time to announce the young man who would win the prestigious award, there were no lights, no music, no fireworks, nor dramatic displays leading up to the announcement. The lack of dramatics separated this ceremony from others I had attended. A man by the name of Dr. Alexander Gabbin took the stage to announce the winner. I had heard Dr. Gabbin speak before and was excited to hear him again. He was a man filled with wisdom, and I waited in anticipation of his speech. He started with scripture, Mark 8: 27: *Jesus, was walking with the disciples towards the villages around Caesarea Philippi when he turned to them and asked, "Who do people say that I am?" It was a simple question, but one that came with much thought. He paused and then asked the question again. His experience as a public speaker was palpable as he spoke to this audience as he allowed the room to absorb the richness of his question. The Disciples replied, "Some say John the Baptist; others say Elijah, and others one of the prophets." Verse 29, "But what about you?" he asked. "Who do you say I am?" It was Peter who responded, "You are the Messiah."*

Dr. Gabbin looked at the young men in front of him. He continued, "Who do people say you are and what is the truth?" The question resounded in a room full of African American men, all of whom were football players. He proceeded to tell the familiar story of 14-year-old Emmitt Till who was murdered because some said he dared to glance and whistle at a white woman. Who did people say Emmitt Till was as a young Black man in that era? They called him a thug, an animal, all because he looked at a white woman.

Dr. Gabbin told of another event in the '50s and asked the same question. Men and women were called criminals and evil because they wanted equal rights. Who did people say that African American men were? He went on to speak on issues we deal with today and the question remains the same, "Who do people say you are?" This question applies to every race. People have been judged throughout history, but for the sake of the men standing in front of him, Dr. Gabbin spoke to the experiences of African Americans.

I sat in awe and anticipation, wondering what he would say next. Then, he did something I had been waiting for all night: he asked each of the past winners and past nominees to stand in front of the crowd. The men lined up from the previous trophy winners to the present, and Dr. Gabbin watched proudly as each of the winners and nominees passed the trophy down, one to the next, until it got to the winner. The men were instructed to say their names, share their GPAs, and the college they went to as they passed it along. The lowest GPA was 3.5. The highest was 4.5. These impressive grades were earned while also doing work in their communities and playing football. When the trophy was passed to the winner,

Dr. Gabbin closed with this statement, "Don't let anyone define you as just a football player. When people ask, 'Who do they say you are?' remember what this trophy stands for and who you are. You are a scholar first, a community servant second, and lastly an athlete. Don't be defined by anything or anyone. You set the definition."

Like many others, I have been called a lot of things, and it is because I let the world define me. My high school coach once called me a loser. He predicted loudly that I would be a loser for the rest of my life. It hurt, and I believed him. While I have no ill will toward him because he was attempting to awaken me to the potential of who I could become, his words had a profound impact on my life. It has been said that hell is paved with good intentions. His words had an impact on me not just because he said them, but because I believed him, and I came dangerously close to letting his words define who I wanted to become.

This book represents a snapshot of my life; a small glimpse into the heart and journey of a high school dropout who went on to attend the University of California at Berkeley and play in the NFL for 11 years. As I look back, these experiences represent my first half. It is easy to go through life feeling like we should be disqualified because of mistakes we have made, or because of the negative comments people have spoken over us, or even because our thoughts are telling us what we can't become.

If we are not careful, we make excuses for why we can't achieve our goals and why we can't go any higher. In effect, we're counting ourselves out. But in my life, I was able to realize that God counted us IN, which matters most.

What does my path from being labeled a loser to making it in the NFL look like? That's the journey I want to describe. Each of us have stories to tell, and each one could be the very thing that someone needs to inspire them to find their greatness inside. I put off writing this book for a long time, despite having the stories in my head and the support of friends and family. The time had to be right, and I had to be ready. I believe my story will light someone else's path, even if it is just one person. It's not where you have been that defines you. Your past will always be a part of you, but it is not who you are.

My mother told me that when I was born, I was stuck in the birth canal for a while. They had to use forceps to help remove me. Because of this, I had a slightly pointed head with scars over my face. I had large eyes and what looked like an extra layer of skin. No one wanted to touch me except my grandmother, who would painstakingly spend time every day trying to mold my head back to normal. That was the beginning of my life as clay being molded into shape. *This is the word that came to Jeremiah from the Lord: "Go down to the potter's house, and there*

I will give you my message." So I went down to the potter's house, and I saw him working at the wheel. But the pot he was shaping from the clay was marred in his hands; so the potter formed it into another pot, shaping it as seemed best to him. (Jeremiah 18:1-4)

1

My Early Life Journey

With nervous anticipation we looked at each other. We were both students and athletes at the University of California Berkeley at the time, and this was the first time we had been asked to do an interview. I was excited because I was with my best friend, and we were both getting our names in the papers. I had done a few small interviews at the junior college where I first attended, but nothing prepared me for an interview at Cal. This was the pinnacle of my life journey. I was a high school dropout and now I attended one of the best public universities in the country. We were being interviewed about the football team and what we saw as the future. My heart was pounding. Don Nobles was my best friend, and his intellect impressed me. I shouldn't have been surprised; after all, he was a Cal student, but so was I. "Are you ready Mr. Nobles?" they asked.

I could tell he was just as nervous as I was. He inhaled deeply and exhaled the negative energy. He seemed to gain control of the situation as they prepared him with the microphone. I recall them asking him what he thought of certain players and the upcoming season. He responded with the grace of a seasoned pro. He had practiced what he was going to say in anticipation of the question and was flawless. I knew what I wanted to say but had only rehearsed an overview in my mind. I thought I knew how to speak to the interviewer and felt I was a natural-born speaker. I was cocky, not realizing that your gifts can only take you so far.

The interviewer turned to me and asked about my life and the future of the team. My reply has become the butt of our joke for the last thirty years. In five minutes, I must have said the word "stepping stone" fifty times. My life has been a series of stepping stones. Attending school is a stepping stone. Our team's continuous growth is a stepping stone. Getting better is a stepping stone. My first interview was a stepping stone. I laugh now whenever I look back but after the interview, we both looked at each other in fear of what the other person thought. 'Stepping stone, huh?' Don asked, looking at me. My life has, indeed, been a stepping stone from one point to the next.

My given name is Kenneth, but I go by Ken. I was soft-spoken when I was young, so when I said "Kenneth" in my shy, quiet tone, people always got it wrong, and so I shortened it to Ken. I'm Ken Harvey, the son of Albert and Carolyn Harvey; brother to Angela, Sherry, Steve, Mike, Irma, and Tomecha Harvey. I was a quiet kid who struggled to find his place in life. I was a very creative child who wanted everyone to get along. I was an empathizer and always tried to see things from the other person's point of view. I can remember times when I felt as though I could truly feel what other people were feeling. It seemed to pour out of them and overflow into my emotions. My father had two jobs; my mother worked when she was not ill. She had shingles at a time when few people were aware of the devastating effects caused by the disease. She endured it while raising seven children. It could have driven anyone insane, but my mother was strong and gave more of herself than she could take in.

I played football since I was a child and had shown some promise, but I wasn't passionate about it at the time. I spent the majority of my time at home watching TV and daydreaming. My parents insisted that I needed to do something other than sitting around, so they enrolled me in football. My coach was a man named Carl Lewis—not the track runner—and he had a heart for helping young men become better men through sports. Too many kids in my neighborhood wandered around aimlessly, getting into trouble because they had nothing else to do. Coach Lewis was an unsung hero who became a second father to many children and helped mold boys into men. My parents signed me up for the team called "The Hornets." If I had any talent, it was the ability to hit. I wasn't a killer all-star, but I wasn't going to back down either. I was a decent player with potential: the result of good genes, a dose of anger, and too much TV. My dad wanted me to play the number one sport in the country and since I didn't have much of a choice, I reluctantly agreed. It got me out of the house, away from the TV, and doing something different. There is a saying that goes, "you do what you know if you don't know any better." I earned the nickname "Hammerhead" because I would go headfirst into the tackle and had a pretty hard head. It was a cool name, but one that I grew to dislike.

Pop Warner Football is a great place for kids to discover who they are. It wasn't the megastar-seeking machine that it is now, but when I played, there were a lot of good players with a future in the NFL. Some were boys in the midst of becoming men. At a young age, I witnessed the growth of some of the greatest athletes. My goal was to make tackles, and I could do that pretty easily, but the job description also included the commitment to get in shape and learn the game. I worked hard in training and began to make a name for myself. Not because I wanted to be great, but because I didn't want to let my teammates down.

While there is a lot of talk about concussions today, I

often think back to the days when I played youth football. We were young boys who were taught to keep going no matter what. If we failed or if we were afraid to get hit, then we were soft, and being soft was no good. A good hit was instant stardom and pats on the back. My actions on the field spoke louder than my words, especially because I was a quiet kid. This was football. People only knew what they knew and so the "kill or be killed" mentality was prevalent throughout these early days for me.

One memory I have is of the drill called "Bull in the Ring." There are several variations of it, but the way I remember was that everyone would get in a circle and there would be one person in the middle. Each person on the outside would be given a number and the coach would call that number out randomly. When your number is called, you would go and attack (try to hit) the person in the middle. The goal of the drill was to have the person in the middle be ready for any type of attack and for those on the outside to be ready when their number is called. We had encircled a guy in the middle, and I'll call him Kyle. Kyle was the one we called "soft" in those days. I'm not sure why he chose to play football, but the goal of any good player was to never show your weakness, never let them know if you are afraid. He showed his hand and fear was all over his body. A number was yelled: "Twenty-three!" Twenty-three came out of nowhere and launched an attack. Kyle was supposed to stand his ground and take the hit. Then, the players would break up and twenty-three would go back to his space on the outside circle. Perhaps this was some ancient warrior training or maybe some military training, but we did the drill and most guys made it through. Kyle did not. He didn't like the hits and he did not want to hit back, and he displayed everything that we were taught that we shouldn't. The coaches fed on it like blood in the waters and started to call out numbers faster, "22," "18," "3." There was no rest and no regrouping. This was football, this was hardcore, and this was a man's sport. Kyle could not take it anymore and did the unthinkable as he took off running, the rest of us standing there, shocked to watch him run away. Bulls don't run, players don't run, and he should not have run. He sprinted for the fence that enclosed the practice facility to make his getaway, and like a mad hunter who had his prey in sight, the coaches unleashed the dogs. He gave us all the order to go after the kid. No holding back; get him. How dare he run in a man's game? We all took off after him and caught him as he was trying to jump the fence to escape. He was hit from all sides, like angry bees we attacked him and when he could no longer hold on to the fence to get over it, he let go and fell to the ground. We did not let up and dove on him like mad bombers, helmets first. I was a mad bomber. I hit him along with others. No one can point a finger and look down on the coaches or us. It was how we practiced. It was football and it was the way things were. We were being toughened up and the weak were being separated.

We were a small team from Austin, Texas, and football in Texas is King. I remember one time we were going to play a team from Dallas. The game does not stand out in my memory except for the fact that we later found out that one of the players on the opposing team was a grown man who was small enough in stature to pass as a child and disguised himself as a little kid playing ball to destroy our team and to win at all costs.

Each of these experiences contributed to my development and understanding of the game of football—and how the culture of football can be either a positive or negative influence. I am lucky that I only have a few examples of these negative experiences, and what I learned in terms of friendship, teamwork, staying off the streets, and having a place to go was priceless. Football was parenting for some kids, and it raised them to be the men they became far more than their parents did. I would not change that part of my life and would do it all over again. I was learning, growing, and developing myself as a person and as a man, and I had seen so many other kids without the benefit of sports that end up in trouble down the road. Carl Lewis was like a second father to me and taught me discipline and teamwork as well as planting the seed of manhood.

My downfall in football goes back to the nickname "Hammerhead." My Pop Warner team was taking a trip to Dallas to play. I had never been further than walking distance from my house let alone out of the state, but there I was going to Dallas with the team. We were going to spend the night there and this was a big moment for me: my first overnight trip. To my horror, I awoke the next morning to soaking wet sheets. It had been a problem in the past, but I was confident it would not happen on this trip because it was not far from home. It did, and I wasn't the only one in my room. Word of this spread quickly, as they do with most kids, and I became known as "Hammerhead, the one who peed the bed" from then on. "Hammerhead, he peed in the bed," became a catchy rhyme and song. If you see me on the street today, please do not address me by that name. It's still a sore spot, and I'm a lot bigger now. My football career in Pop Warner came to an end. At that point, I was happy if I never had anything to do with football again. One of the simplest ways to stuff potential is to attack it early and kill it before it has a chance to develop. Many of our youth's potential or seeds of greatness are never planted firmly enough or given a chance to grow. In the end, I was a small flower that snuck through a crack of hard concrete. My fate as a football player was yet to be determined, but at the time, I was known as "Hammerhead, who peed in the bed."

That same day Jesus went out of the house and sat by the lake. Such large crowds gathered around him that he got into a boat and sat in it, while all the people stood on the shore. Then he told them many things in parables, saying: "A farmer went out to sow his seed. As he was scattering the seed, some fell along the path, and the birds came and ate it up. Some fell on rocky places, where it did not have much soil. It sprang up quickly because the soil was shallow. But when the sun came up, the plants were scorched, and they withered because they had no root. Other seeds fell among thorns, which grew up and choked the plants. Still, other seeds fell on good soil, where it produced a crop a hundred, sixty, or thirty times what was sown. Whoever has ears, let them hear." (St. Matthew 13:1-9 – NIV)

2

Who Am I

In Genesis 30, Jacob a servant to Laban asked for the spotted and striped sheep from the stock of Laban's sheep. Those were the ones considered inferior and weak with little value. Jacob knew that God was on his side. It was said that every time the pure sheep would mate with a striped one, Jacob would put a stripe or spotted piece of wood before their eyes. They would then produce a striped or spotted offspring. They produced what they saw. That is often how we are today; we produce what we see.

Sex, crime, hate, greed, fear: we produce what we see before us. I was a confusing combination of rage bottled up in a person who didn't want to hurt anyone, so I took my frustration out on the things around me. Our house had holes I punched in the walls and broken items that resulted from my angry tantrums. I was like the Incredible Hulk. I loved that show because it reflected how I saw myself. I would faithfully sit in front of the TV and watch the show over and over and over. No one could understand the monster inside. The real me was the quiet intellect trying to express himself.

As the sting of my past embarrassment in football faded, I returned to the football field in high school. We had some good players, and I played fullback and linebacker. Football to me entails training, and training brings about strength. I was strong and began to build muscle. I thought I had the super-human strength of my superhero doppelgänger, the Hulk. To understand the Hulk, you must first understand the Hulk's alter ego. The same could be said of me. I used to watch a lot of educational TV shows when I was younger. It was both a blessing and a curse. I had lost interest in school. I already knew a lot of what they were teaching from watching TV shows, but the issue was that television is more about the assimilation of information than training myself to learn. I was smart, but I lacked the discipline to sit down and study. Without discipline and hard work, I was only an illusion or a 30-minute TV show that had no depth. I learned the answers from memory or what I saw, not by doing the work to get the answers myself. That gift, combined with shyness, taught me how to finesse my way through classes. It was the Ken Harvey Show. However, I reached a point where I could no longer do that, and I began to fall behind.

The Ken Harvey show continued as I was a lover of *Star Trek* and *The Twilight Zone*. My mind was set on the "What if's" of possibilities. I saw worlds and people that I would never know on *Star Trek*. It gave me a vision that anything was possible. Someday, we would be there; someday, I might be there. My favorite character was Mr. Spock. He had struggles, too; he fought to control himself just like I did. I knew there was more out there, and I was determined to find a way to achieve it. A lot of what I have now is based on what I saw as a young kid growing up. In *The Twilight Zone*, I loved the twist, the perceived notions of what was turned on its head and then found out to be something else. I saw something similar in the way I felt about myself, and it gave me the power to look at the other side, to think about the potential flip side. I also liked the old TV show *Kung Fu*. In most karate movies, there is a great comeback when someone who was initially defeated went on to master techniques that make them invincible. I watched *Kung Fu* and learned values, but also wanted to be like these characters. I wanted to be able to control my mind and not feel any pain. I believed it was possible and committed myself to the point where I would go outside and hit a tree with my fist, believing that I could control the pain and block it out. When I was spanked or punished by my parents, I treated it as an internal test of will, to see how much I could endure without crying out. I was Kung Fu. I had trained my mind to deal with pain, to take it and to persevere. I attempted to become what I saw. I now understand why so many commercials and movies include the disclaimer, "Do not try this at home."

In elementary school, I watched a show called *The Odd Couple*. There was a skit where Felix or Oscar told the other not to assume. He then went on to say, "If you assume, you make an 'ass' out of 'u' and 'me'." I thought that was brilliant the way they twisted the word around. I couldn't wait to use that on someone. It had been a week since I had seen the show, and I remember sitting in class when a girl said the magic word. I was ready and primed to say what I had been taught. I looked at her with a smile on my face and then blurted out the words. *What was the worst that could happen?* I thought. I stepped out of the comfort of my shy life to throw out some words of wisdom. The young lady looked at me and then slapped me hard across the face. It was both loud and painful. I remember looking at her in disbelief, wondering what the hell had just happened. How did I go from imparting knowledge to getting slapped across the face? To make matters worse, the teacher and the entire class heard it. The teacher approached me and yelled, "What did you say?" His face was red. I shrank in his presence and timidly repeated what I had said. I didn't see anything wrong with it, but everyone else did. "You," he yelled, "go over there and apologize to that girl."

"I'm sorry, please forgive me," I said, my voice shaking. She gave me the "Whatever" and "That is what you deserve" look before dismissing me. The teacher told me to grab my chair and sit in the far corner of the room until class was over. I sat with my head down, facing the crowd, trying to comprehend what had just happened. That experience taught me to never step out of my comfort zone because if I did it could be painful.

I was in fifth grade at a school located in east Austin. We had a couple of bullies that ruled the classrooms and tried to rule the school. They wanted to be one of the toughest schools in the country. The school served predominately Black students in a Black neighborhood but had mostly white teachers. The teachers worked to help shape students who knew nothing beyond their environment. We even had a teacher who would take a group of kids from Austin to Dallas to visit an amusement park once a year. It may seem like a small thing, but for those who had never been outside their small environment, it was a big deal.

The bullies decided to create classroom wars in which one room would fight against another. It was war, and anyone from another classroom who gets caught became the victim. They were young bullies trying to create something they had seen somewhere else. I was just a guy trying to please others and had gotten to the point where my teacher liked me and had given me the responsibility of delivering papers to the classroom next door. I was even given the honor of taking down the American flag.

Delivering the papers was a good job with no perks, and I enjoyed it because it showed that the teachers trusted me. Unfortunately, I had to bring these papers to the classroom that we were warring with. Most people didn't participate in the battles, but some did. It was something the bullies were trying to implant, and there were a few who believed in this philosophy. These students saw me as the enemy because I didn't believe or partake in the battle. I went to deliver the paper to a classroom where a small white teacher sat at her desk, and I felt some relief as I was sure that she would be there to protect me. I walked into the room and quickly put the papers on the desk.

As I turned to leave, a large student closed the door, and I froze. I didn't want to get into a fight; I didn't even like fighting. In my mind, I was still that superhero and if I unleashed my powers, someone could get hurt. I thought if I fought someone, I would actually kill them, and I was also afraid. The door was still closed as I stood face to face with someone whose mission was to take me down. He didn't know me, and it didn't matter. He was only in school because he had to be. I stood there looking at him not sure what to do. He was staring at me as though I stole something from his mother.

In the blink of an eye, before I could call for help, he kicked me between the legs. The pain was excruciating, making me go down on my knees. The teacher yelled out for him to stop, but it was too late. You can't reverse pain. Tears streamed from my eyes. I ran out of the room doubled over, crying, and breathing hard. It was easy to see why some kids hated school. I was quickly becoming one of them. I limped away, vowing to never deliver papers to that classroom again without an escape route.

The classroom wars finally ended after an event with a kid from a rival classroom. He was alone; I and five other guys saw him. Two of us were not troublemakers, but the other three were. They proceeded to beat the kid up. I stood by and watched it happen, which made me guilty by association. The school finally became aware of the battles and the staff was on high alert. They broke up the fight and gathered us together to be disciplined.

The administration was going to put a stop to these wars, starting with us. At that time, schools could administer physical discipline but still had to get the parent's permission to do so. I remembered them calling my dad and asking if it was okay to punish me. He told them if I was involved, I should be punished. While we all sat in a room waiting for our punishment, one of the guys who seemed bigger than the rest of us was first in line. I remember his mom coming in, she was a large woman, large from both a child's and an adult's perspective. She came in with rollers in her hair and blood in her eyes. She looked around the room at her son and then at us. "Can I discipline him?" she said as the teachers looked at each other in a bit of shock and then agreed. She took him to another room, and I swear I heard the wind from the belt as it flew through the air. He screamed and yelled as she brought the lighting of the living God on his body. I could hear him running like a caged animal trying to get free. We all started to cry for fear that she would punish all of us. That was enough to scare me straight. She came out of the room sweating after inflicting much pain. There's a fuzzy line between discipline and child abuse in those days, but even then, from my perspective, it was child abuse. And although he was wrong in his actions, I could see why he was such a troubled kid. We were next in line. My eyes were still watering when they declared that she would not be the one punishing us. I breathed a sigh of relief. We would either be punished by the school or our parents. My dad was at work and could not take the time off to come to the school, so he let the teachers do it. We were in the principal office and the principal had a paddle. I stood facing him and I heard my teacher and another teacher saying, "We're so disappointed in you," and then I was told to bend over. The principal positioned himself behind me with the paddle and then wound up and unleashed my punishment. I was bent over facing my disappointed teachers while being spanked from behind. "Deal with the pain," I told myself. This moment is the one I remembered whenever I saw the inkling of a bully after that; I did not want to be around one and I certainly did not want to be one.

I had some artistic talent as a child, or at least I thought I did. I could draw what I saw but I had difficulty with the details or understanding the principles of drawing. I had a natural ability to draw but was not committed enough to hone my skills and spend the time learning how to be better. I wanted to be an artist and once drew what I thought would be my masterpiece, my work of art. I took the picture to a friend of mine and a girl that was with him. I was trying to impress her as well with my skills. She looked at the picture, and then she looked at me and she shrugged, "You're ugly, but at least you can draw." Her comments hurt. No matter how well I drew, it did not change the way that anyone saw me. It truly broke me. A teardrop spilled over and fell on the art, mixing the charcoal and ruining the picture. I didn't want to be an artist any longer.

I was shaped by what I saw and what was in front of me. Some kids grow out of it, others build on it, and a lot of it stuck to me.

Another comic book character that I admired was Thor. I wanted to be as noble as he was because he was one of the strongest Marvel characters; he had to learn some hard lessons along with his great strength. I liked his undying loyalty for the earth, which he adopted and would do anything to protect. My biggest disappointment came when I found out the real Thor in Norse mythology was a redhead, and though I still loved the character I wondered why he was portrayed as a Blonde-haired demi-god?

There were not a lot of African American heroes to look up to in those days besides athletes, and in the comic books even fewer. The Falcon, a sidekick of Captain America, had no real powers. Power Man, who was strong and streetwise, had been wrongly convicted of a crime he did not commit and so had come from prison. On TV, I had *Good Times* with a strong father character, but they were still poor and just trying to make it. The father ended up getting killed on the show, which just reinforced negative stereotypes. There was *The Jeffersons*, who had made it, but their success seemed so far away and was always a comedy. Other movies and shows featured the Black cast, but their roles were often stereotypes and token roles.

My favorite musical entertainer was Prince. Prince was my mentor; I wanted to become part of his world. Who would not want to be an international lover? If it wasn't going to happen in real life, I could at least think about it. I was a young man learning about sex and what better teacher than Prince.

His lessons were taught through "Little Red Corvette 1999," "Horny Toad," "Lady Cab driver," "D.M.S.R," "Automatic," "All the Critics Love You in New York," and "International Lover." Another favorite song of mine was "Under Pressure" by Queen. I still listen to it today because I identify so closely with the way I feel whenever I am under pressure and about to explode.

People are the most violent at home, or with those closest to them. I was a quick-tempered person, but only where there would be no opposition, or where I didn't care what people thought of me. I wasn't a violent kid who would beat up family members, but I did vent my anger in my home, and looking back now I feel embarrassed by the amount of damage I caused.

In life, we all have a unique story that shapes who we are. The same circumstances can have different effects on different people. I only mentioned a few examples from my own life, but there are many more. We often become a product of our environment, a product of what people say about us, a product of what we see, and it helps shape us into becoming who we are. I was becoming a product of what I saw and what I believed about myself, just like Jacob placing the sticks in front of the lambs and producing what they saw.

3

I Was Confused and Lost

I got good at blocking things out, ignoring pain, and not dealing with issues; my karate movies paid off. I was able to block out what I perceived as pain and internalize what I had to endure. My mom tried to discipline me with a belt, and I would take it as if nothing touched me, which frustrated her, but she let me know that I was winning. I would look her in the eyes and smile. I still feared my father, however, as he could surpass my threshold for ignoring the pain. Avoiding things had become my habit, a way of life for me. As a result, I don't recall much of my childhood. I ignored a lot of what was going on and blocked out some events. I built my prison by choosing to surround myself with walls that shut out anything that I did not want to deal with.

There were many good things in my life as well. My

cousin and I have our birthdays around the same time, the 11th and 6th of the same month respectively. Sometimes we celebrated our birthdays together, which was a lot of fun. I was very competitive with my brothers when we played football, basketball, or some other made-up game. We all wanted to win. We once broke a guy's collarbone while playing football. He thought he was tougher than the Harveys, but we proved him wrong. I remember that I almost got hit by a train as I played chicken with the oncoming train and my brother came to my rescue when I got caught on a spike. I remember getting chased by our dog; once he started chasing us, he would get into a rage, and he would lose control and try to bite us. We had to outrun him. It was no fun getting bit, but we always found the fun in outrunning him and knew that he was helping us increase our speed.

I remember playing softball at school. I was in the outfield and had no idea what I was doing. Suddenly, there was a hit, and the ball flew high into the sky. I saw it and knew it was coming down on me. I put up my glove to catch it, but I missed, and the ball hit me on the bridge of my nose, possibly because of the pressure of knowing everyone was watching me combined with my lack of confidence in my softball abilities. It was painful, and tears welled up in my eyes. "Take the pain, deal with it, and don't let them see you cry," I said to myself. Everyone asked if I was okay, and I said yes, even though I wasn't. I sucked it up. My training paid off.

The very next play the same thing happened. The ball hit me in the nose again. At that moment, all of my toughness vanished, and I felt as if I had broken both my nose and my resolve at the same time. This made a lasting impression on me, and even impacted my experiences in the NFL. I only have a couple of recorded interceptions in my entire career with the NFL. Because I never pushed through my fear and dealt with these experiences, whenever anything (even as a football) came close to my face I would panic, tumbling into the fear I felt when I got hit in the nose with the softball. This truly convinced me of the saying, "if you don't deal with an issue, it will always be an issue." I never did, it always was, and I predict that I will still flinch and panic when something unexpected comes at me.

I have a hard time remembering the time when I dropped out of school. Memories can be foggy, both by the circumstances in which they were created, and also pushed away intentionally. For me, painful memories are pushed the furthest away, and I had to force myself to investigate my mind and piece together my experiences to learn from them and make myself aware of why and how they impacted my life. It's an interesting thing to have to investigate your own life, to approach it as an outsider, because that is honestly how I felt when I began. I began my inquiry into my own life by finding out when I graduated from high school. I don't think I ever looked at my degree, even when I first got it. I kept that part of my life locked away and tried hard never to think about it once it was over. I closed that chapter and threw it away because it was easier to do that than to relive the pain I felt. I learned never to deal with things that caused me discomfort, and this has been a prevailing issue in my life, even to this day. I knew I graduated six months late, so instead of finishing with my class in the Spring of 1983, I had to wait until January of 1984. There was no walking with my class, no getting my cap and gown, no pats on the back with people saying how proud they were of me. I was a man in purgatory, stuck somewhere in between. This verse was used, and it puzzled me:

"When an impure spirit comes out of a person, it goes through arid places seeking rest and does not find it. Then it says, 'I will return to the house I left.' When it arrives, it finds the house unoccupied, swept clean, and put in order. Then it goes and takes with it seven other spirits more wicked than itself, and they go in and live there. And the final condition of that person is worse than the first. That is how it will be with this wicked generation." (St. Matthew 12:43-45).

As I got older, this Bible verse started to make a lot more sense. I came to realize that when you choose not to deal with something, it is not truly gone, but returns with a lot more baggage than when you began. Only God can truly cleanse us of our sins. For example, people who never learn to deal with emotions grow older, and because they are older, people often expect them to have found ways to manage their emotions. Instead of finding positive ways to cope with challenging emotions, some people begin to drink or use drugs to escape, and now emotions are intensified by additional issues related to the effects of drinking or abusing drugs, like health problems that stem from the stress and substance abuse. They may be arrested for DUI, or maybe they have other issues that continue to compound. I had to confront some issues that I thought were long resolved while writing this book. I had to face them and make some adjustments. We frequently do not recognize the demons we face, and as a result, we continue to be attacked without knowing where the attack is coming from.

I talk a lot about fighting the invisible man in my speeches. The punches come fast and furious, and you often don't know where they're coming from, but if you study the bruises, patterns, and habits, you can figure out where they're coming from and, over time, build a defense against them. The first step I took to confront the invisible man was to write to my old school and request my transcript. It was time to accept myself for who I was. I'd gotten pretty good at hiding, running, and locking things away in compartments. Now was the time to open the door and take a look. I wrote and called my old high school to obtain my high school records. It was a difficult decision, but in retrospect, it was a simple one. All I had to do was pick up the phone, but I was nervous. When you spend your entire life learning how to avoid situations, even the simplest tasks become difficult. I called to see if they still had my transcript, and to my surprise, they did. All I had to do was send three dollars, and they would send it to me. That seemed simple enough, but I understand how difficult it can be to take the first step at times. Football is great because coaches force you to do something. Winning will push you to continue, but if you don't know how to push yourself, once those outside forces are gone, you are left having to face yourself in the mirror. If the issues aren't dealt with, they come back stronger.

When I finally received my transcript, the illusion that I was a good student was confirmed as a misconception. I did not put any effort into studying. I was smart but being smart and doing something with it are two different things. The gifts I had at a younger age were now gone. School was no longer about the things I had seen on TV and could translate into the classroom, but more about studying and studying habits. I had none and even though my parents tried to push me to study, I was dead set against it.

There is a book called *Good to Great* that talks about how we settle for just being good, which hampers us from becoming great. I don't know if I was unmotivated, but being super smart was not something prized at our schools. I think it was more a combination of a lot of things, but if you did not learn to study and you are okay with just getting by with low standards, then you become a victim of the law of attractions. I had no educational goals. I kept to myself, so it was easy to hide in broad daylight. In the end, I got what I put into it. In high school, if you are gifted in football, it's not a pass, but a chance to get by, and that is what I did. It's almost embarrassing to look at the classes I took, but at least I did get an A in football.

My question to you is, who are your heroes? Who are the people you look up to? In my time, all our heroes were athletes or entertainers. Being smart was something frowned upon, not something we emulated. My dad could only teach me what was taught to him by his dad. Slavery is an evil tool. If it is not recognized and dealt with, it could have lasting effects that go on from generation to generation, unleashing new demons that go along with it. I had bad grades, but I was passing and at the same time becoming a good football player. Internal anger had an outlet, and I was blessed with good genes, so the combination was letting me get by. I also wanted to please people, and this pushed me to work harder for the coaches and my friends. Gaining acceptance from football allowed me to fit in, to become a part of the images that I saw on TV. I wanted to be like "Ed Too Tall Jones," a defensive end for the Dallas Cowboys. I wanted to be a football player and dominate the field.

I wanted to make my father proud in the only way I knew how. The Hulk was now an Avenger, a part of a team, and my anger was no longer a curse, but a blessing. I could be as mad as I wanted and take it out on the person across from me.

Do you see the problem? Sooner or later time bombs explodes. I was creating the right mixture. I was a shy type and didn't talk much. I held everything in; I was angry because I felt people did not understand me which frustrated me. I was falling behind in my classes. I was a diamond in the rough that was unmined, so the pressure to live up to that potential was getting to me. In the end, I was lost. I started missing school; it was easy because both parents were working. I would miss, write a note, and sign their name to it. I was smart enough to get by and the standard was low for an African American kid from my neighborhood. Getting by was acceptable. The only problem with my grand plan was playing football. I had to go to school. My loophole was that football classes were at the end of the day. If I went to some classes and missed others, none of the coaches would be the wiser, or at least that is what I thought. I could still feel like a superhero and not let anyone down. I thought I was having my cake and eating it, too.

I did this for a while and thought I had mastered the great art of getting away with something, not knowing that I was just digging myself deeper in a hole, feeding the negative patterns and starving the good ones. I started missing a lot of classes. I would miss a day and I would be embarrassed that I missed that day, not wanting to face up to the fact, so I would miss another one. What would I do with my free time? I was at home watching TV. I lived through fantasies and from there I would teach myself. How do you develop attention deficit disorder? Constantly go from show to show. I found a way to slip between the cracks and become unnoticed. *But then; this sin will become for you like a high wall, cracked and bulging, that collapses suddenly, in an instant.* (Isaiah 30:13.NIV).

4

Time to Pay the Piper

My small world of football was starting to become a problem. I started missing days of weightlifting in the off-season, and occasionally a practice here and there. My last place of refuge was slipping away and now even the coaches were losing hope in me. I used to not understand what fear of success meant, but I was living it. I was afraid to become as good as I could be. Now I understood that lack of confidence was a breeding ground for fear. Hence, I begin to sabotage the one thing that could get me out of the world that I was in. My life trickled down to a moment where a decision had to be made. The coaches knew I had the potential to be good, so they wanted to help me. They offered to adjust my class schedule to make things easier. I, on the other hand, was frustrated that they wanted to put me in easy classes just so I could pass. I was smart!!! I just didn't show it. When it rains, it pours and so my parents had found out about the forged notes and missing days in school, and they got on me. This was the moment in my life that I was to become either the Hulk or David Banner. I was left with few choices: drop out of school, continue school to get straight Fs, or take the easy classes and let the coaches do their work. I chose to drop out of school because I felt I needed time to think, to figure out what I wanted to do with my life. I wasn't dumb; I was just lost and didn't have a focus. Dropping out would allow me to think and decide what I wanted to do. Looking back, it is easy to understand why my coaches would have had such a hard time with me. I had all the potential in the world, but it was wasted. Before I dropped out of school, while preparing to play football, I was growing in my natural gifts. I was becoming stronger. Even when I missed days of school, I was still gaining strength doing pushups at home or lifting things around the house, and because of that, I was a bad influence. I never thought that I was disruptive, but now in my later years, I could see that I was setting an example that it's okay not to lift, to not do the right thing and you still would be successful. I see how one person could bring everyone else down with bad behavior.

Though I looked like an average high school football player I felt bigger. I had turned my anger into something productive by lifting weights. Instead of hitting the walls in my house or breaking things, my anger went toward the weight room. I cringe when I hear about states wanting to take out afterschool activities or physical education because this may be the only chance for some kids to work off that extra energy; a way for them to direct what could become negatives to positives. Studies have also shown the value of physical activity in education.

I told my parents that I was going to drop out of school. They were deeply hurt but continued to love me. I have good parents. As parents working several jobs you only have so much time to devote to one child. My dad simplified the situation when he said, "Boy, you are way too big to be sitting on your butt and doing nothing but watching TV, you need to get a job or join the military and you need to do something sooner rather than later." I was still a kid even though I was bigger and could have easily turned to drugs or crime but that was not me. I was still the quiet kid who thought very little of himself. I was like Gideon, the least among his brethren. It was after dropping out of school. My escape was once again the gym. I would work out like a mad man; I could be as mad as I wanted to but at the end of the day, I would see some results. The people in the gym were my friends and I was one of them— the bodybuilder group. I already had some size from football, but now there was real gain. The more I went, the better I felt. I focused on doing my arms. Guns for the girls, right? But I had no girls. I thought I could be as quiet as I wanted, and girls would still want to talk to me because of my arms. I worked my arms like a mad man and with my genetic potential, I saw explosive growth. I began to walk around with a sense of pride in me.

Eventually, I started to look funny with big arms and nothing else, so I began the process of trying to get the rest of my body to match the bulging arms. I started working on the bench press and was getting stronger by the day. I never did steroids but had the benefit of working out with guys who knew a lot about weights. They pushed me beyond my mental limitations. I met one guy who must have been about 260 pounds. He was trying out for pro football at the time, and he would always give me advice. I met another gentleman who was paralyzed from the waist down but was benching way more than guys twice his size. They were my family in the gym and so I worked, listened to instructions, and went from benching 200 pounds to 300 pounds.

I was now looking like the comic book characters that I loved so much: I was Thor, I was the Hulk, and I was Samson from the Bible. I realized that when you believe in something and put in the work, it opens realms of possibilities. I became what I saw. At the gym, I saw bodybuilders who had size and knowledge. I saw images on the wall of what I could be. In a way, I could be that superhero, but I also realized later in life that it was just an image and images of you have no foundation. They are only a drawing, a piece of paper, and a quick flash. There was no substance; I was an image but still was lacking in a foundation.

Over time, I developed nicely. I was eating like a horse and lying around the house doing nothing but watching TV and going to the gym. I was so busy looking at the role model that I wasn't much of one for my brothers and sisters. I remember getting mad at my younger brother Steve because he was disciplined enough to sit down and read the Bible. I wanted that discipline and coveted what he had and what I didn't have. I was in my fifties before I finally understood why I used to get mad at him. The reason being I was coveting what I didn't have or didn't believe I had. My covetousness turned to anger. If you follow the comments on the internet, you will see that we live in a society that covets what people have and celebrates when they fall.

I was that type. *What shall we say, then? Is the law sinful? Certainly not! Nevertheless, I would not have known what sin was had it not been for the law. For I would not have known what coveting really was if the law had not said, "You shall not covet." But sin, seizing the opportunity afforded by the commandment,* produced *in me every kind of coveting.* (Romans 7:7-8)

My parents kept on me about getting a job. I looked in

the papers to see what type of job a dropout could get. I had previously worked in the fast-food industry as a cook but even that had been tainted. I was fired for being young and stupid, and for stealing. Trying to please people and not standing up for myself was a recipe for disaster. I started off taking a few steaks after work thinking nothing of the cost to the owner. The owner was not there and while we had managers, we still found ways to steal. It pains me as I write this, but I was a thief. It starts with taking one pack of steaks and not getting caught, then another. You take a few more and it becomes easier. I got to a point where I was taking a decent amount of food home. My parents thought that I was paying for it, so I was in the clear. I finally realized what I was doing was wrong, but the train was moving.

Some new guys started working with me, just as I was starting to stop. They started taking a few steaks home at first, but then cases. I saw what they were doing and knew it was wrong, but I did nothing. I was out of the game and had concluded that I would no longer steal so I assumed I had washed my hands of my wrongdoing and would be a good employee. A guy who used to work at the restaurant came and asked me to get him some steaks for a party. I told him I was out of the game, but he persisted, so I gave in. I told him it was only going to be one more time and then I would be done. We set up the pickup outside the store near a large dumpster. I would place the steaks there after work and he would come to pick them up. The deed was done, and I thought I was free. One day at the end of work as we were closing, I saw the manager come in and he called me to the back. I knew I had been set up when I saw the guy that I was supposed to be getting the meat for standing right next to the manager. Running was not an option, the manager stood blocking my path with a metal rod at his side. I was smart enough to know better, not because I couldn't take him but because he was right, and I was busted. The owner was a large round man, but he was just as scared as I was. He was shaking and I could see it. He looked at me, "Kenneth, I know you are a good kid and you've not been taking all this meat by yourself. I want you to tell me who has been taking the meat." I played dumb. I was protecting people who didn't care about me. He asked a few more questions and still, I said nothing. This is when I knew I had favor from the Lord because things could have gone in any direction. Perhaps I could have run and he would have tried to stop me. I would have gotten into a fight with him and would have won. I was Hulk; he was fat. The police would have been called and I would be thrown in jail and lost in the system. Maybe he had a gun, and I could have made a move toward him; he would pull out the gun and I would be a dead thief. His life and store could have been ruined and I would be a corpse. Instead, he told me to leave his store and not to come back. Sometimes we have favor in our lives without really knowing it. God was watching over me.

I later found a job at McDonald's. It used to be the type of job to start a working career. You got paid minimum wages, but it was a start while you were in high school or before you went off to college. It was the first step and sometimes a second chance. I remember the owner sitting me down and asking me why I left the last job. He told me he called, and they said that I was banned from the store, so I told him why I was banned. He looked at me and said that I seemed like a good kid, and he was willing to take a chance on me. That was a favor. I started to work at McDonald's as my second career. I was a likable person, quiet, hardworking, and polite. I did my job and tried to be the best cook. The same demons from my past came up differently. I had not trained myself to be a good student and only relied on my natural ability. I could flip a burger like a crazy man, handling the lunch hour's blitz by myself. A job that would normally take two people, I would do it alone. There came opportunities to grow within the company. I simply had to study and take a test to open the door for an opportunity to move up. My pride and my lack of being a good student got in the way. I felt as though I deserved any promotion there was because I worked the hardest so I should be next in line automatically. They kept telling me to study and take the test, but I did not. My pride and ego got in the way, so I had a chip on my shoulder when others around me came in after me and were promoted because they studied and took the test. I became angry and quiet. Can you see the pattern of my life? This was the very thing that God had been trying to teach me. It was easier to blame everyone else for my mistakes. I was mad at McDonald's, mad at everyone, when I should have been mad at myself because it was my fault.

I could have taken the test, worked my way up and one day owned my own McDonald's. There were a lot of fast-food franchises looking for minorities and offering packages to help with ownership. All these opportunities passed by because I had not learned from the first lesson, and I blamed everyone instead of dealing with it myself.

Once again, I was out of a job. I felt as though I had no purpose in life, so I began to look in the papers for another job and could not find one. There were sales jobs, get-rich-quick type of jobs but nothing that I wanted or felt was worth me trying. I thought most of them were scams, so instead of doing something, I sat around at home and did nothing.

Everyone's fuse was short each time I lost my temper, and the fuses continued to get shorter. I remember fighting my dad and wrestling him to the floor. In my mind, I was being noble by not hurting him. In everyone else's mind, I was attacking dad. They turned on me when I felt that I was the one in the right. My only savior during that time was a black lab that my dad picked up from the animal shelter. I remember getting so mad that I started to run away, but the dog would follow. I would throw rocks at him to keep him away, but he would follow keeping his distance. I would yell at him, but he would keep following until I stopped to think about what I was doing and where I was going. And then I realized I was going nowhere. I had nothing, so I ended up going back home and my dog followed. A dog is God backward.

The pressure started to build, and I couldn't fight it anymore. My anger turned into depression. My dad wanted me to join the military, and again I said no. I did not want to take his advice or listen to him because in my mind he was partially the cause of my anger. It didn't make sense, but what does to an irrational child. I didn't want to look in the mirror, but I had to. I was afraid of my reflection. I was this big kid, who had dropped out of high school, who still worried about what everyone thought of me. Seeing their faces once they found out I had dropped out, I knew they all thought I was dumb, and I hated that. I was not dumb.

This created more blame, more shame, more feeling of loneliness, and a chip on my shoulder. Working out at the gym meant nothing anymore because I was going nowhere with my strength. I was like a man locked up in prison for life, lifting weights for no purpose other than to waste time.

The day came when I was at my lowest when I felt that

the world would be better off without me. I felt that everyone believed I was worthless. I had a thought that if I killed myself the world would be a much better place without me. No one would miss me, and everyone would move on. Self-pity fueled the fire in me to quit. It is amazing when I look back—things weren't as bad as they seemed, but at the moment it felt like death was my only option. I took a bottle of my mother's pills, though I wasn't sure what kind of pills they were, but I figured they would do the trick. Nothing happened. Darn those superhero powers. I tried again, this time swallowing a bottle of lighter fluid. Again, nothing happened except when it came out the other way, you probably could have thrown a match in the toilet and it would have exploded. I tried one more time and again, nothing happened. I was frustrated with life and frustrated with not being able to take my own life. I felt I was terrible at doing that, too. Since I did not die, nor felt any effects of what I was doing, I kept quiet about it. I never even said anything to my parents until way later in my life.

Me surviving was the turning point in my life. I got to my knees one night, crying out to God to give me a path, give me some direction. I told God that if He did, I would honor His name and that I would give Him all the glory. I was never much of a church guy; in fact, I disliked church. I thought it was fake and merely a show. We would go on Sundays, and it felt like a fashion show. People would dress in their Sunday best and look down on you if you weren't dressed as well. I believed they were just playing church. I never knew the Holy Spirit, but I would see the same people get in spirit every week. I wondered what it all meant and at times I hated it because I did not have it. My grandparents lived right next door to the church and were the closest thing I knew to what the Christian life should look like. My Grandparents embraced us, and we saw who Christ was through them. I prayed for God's help and eventually felt as if God was saying that I had a purpose for my life and there was a reason He did not allow me to die. I felt there was something for me to do. I had a direction, a focus, and a destiny.

Now I was on fire because I realized I had a purpose. When you feel like you have a purpose, it gives you energy. I felt like going back to school, then to college. I wanted to prove to everyone that I was not stupid, I had a brain and now I was ready to show it. I was still the same quiet person, but I was different. The devil almost had me. He planted seeds of doubt and insecurity. Who do men say I am? Don't matter. I was a child of God with a purpose.

5

The Purpose and the Plan

I was now a child of God with a purpose. I prayed and God answered. Now I needed to create a plan. If I wanted to get into college, which I figured would be a hard task, I had to go back to school. I ran or hid from everything and now I had to go back and face the past. There was renewed confidence through my revelation with God, but I was still scared. Along the way, God sent people into my life to confirm what He told me. They were random people that I would run into. They would tell me I was too big and had too much going for me to be a dropout. There was a time I would get offended by these comments, but now I saw them as advice. Some encouraged me to get back in school, so after taking a semester off, I made a choice. I went back to school. "But the word is very near you, in your mouth and your heart, that you may observe it. *"See, I have set before you today life and prosperity, and death and adversity; in that, I command you today to love the LORD your God, to walk in His ways and to keep His commandments and His statutes and His judgments, that you may live and multiply, and that the LORD your God may bless you in the land where you are entering to possess it.* (Deuteronomy 30:15)

The decision to go back to school was the first step of choosing life. I had to humble myself by going back and facing everyone. It was hard, because of my size and what I thought everyone thought of me, but when you have a purpose, a goal, and the fire to act with that goal, you push past the looks and the stares and into the promise. I went back and dealt with it. I enrolled in school and thought everything would be perfect, but I was wrong. I went back to my football coach and wanted to play football again. I thought all would be forgiven and things would go back to the way it was, but it did not. His reply surprised me. He was the coach who told me I was a loser, and I was going to be a loser all my life. It hurt. There was no one else there as a witness, and I am sure he would have denied saying such a thing, but that's what I heard. I walked away with my tail between my legs. I was bent, but not broken, because I still had a purpose and a vision, and his words had become my fuel. *Where there is no vision, the people perish: but he that keepnet the law, happy is he.* (Proverbs 29:18).

I didn't know it at the time, but part of God's master

plan was His call to humility. He allows us to face challenges that provoke us to repent from where we were, so we can step into where we need to go. I could have responded with anger and hate, but I was surrounded by peace (and a bit of I'm going to show you.) I continued with school, and I was now about 220 pounds of muscle and looked like an older college person. As crazy as it sounds, I tried to blend in and become invisible. As a man thinks, so is he, right? I had a purpose, but it was not something that I stepped boldly into. I went to class, just trying to figure out how to make it through. The words of the coach rang in my ears, and I thought maybe he was right. There is a book I read later in life called *The Power of Habit* by Charles Duhigg. The author spoke about habits we create and how they are developed in your brain. My habit was to hide and run away. The destiny God laid out for me was covered with condemnation and fear, so I tried to be invisible. I was very much like Saul whom God choose to rule over Israel, but when the announcement was made that he would be the king, he hid. I did the same thing, afraid to claim my rightful place. Then I realized God has a way of throwing out messages in whispers, hoping you hear. He continues to do this for a while, but eventually, the whisper becomes a yell.

I felt alone and by myself in high school but remembered running into a janitor. There was nothing special about him. He did his job and he did it well. I spoke with him once and he told me about all the things he should have or could have done, but the fact is, he was still sweeping floors. I got the message. There is nothing wrong with sweeping floors, but if your life is full of regrets, then you are missing something. I vowed I would never be that guy. God whispered through someone else, and I heard. I got motivated and finished up school, absorbing the pain and compartmentalizing it. I put it into a dark place, never to be seen. I graduated but did not get to see my diploma. I just wanted out. I still had the vision of doing something with my life, but I was not sure what it was going to be. I just knew I had to get to college to prove everyone wrong. I wasn't stupid and I wasn't dumb.

I was now eighteen and played basketball almost every night with friends and soon I became a better athlete. From my parent's perspective, I was still lazy, sucking up food and using up money they could not afford to spend. I fought with my brothers, dad, sisters, and mother. The home had become a battleground and I left signs of war all over the place; holes in the wall, broken furniture, and destroyed relationships. I finally got a job at Fuddruckers cooking steak and flipping burgers. I had the big arms of a grown, well-trained muscle man, but inside, I was still a kid. It was time to get out. It wasn't my choice, but the law was laid, and I needed to do something. While working at the restaurant, I heard repeatedly, "What are you going to do with your life? You are too big to be just flipping steaks; you can do so much more." I began telling everyone about my dream of going to college. The Bible talks about speaking things that are not as if they were and that is what I was doing. I was going to college. They looked at the facts and I could understand the blank look that came on their faces when I told them what I was going to do. I was a kid who had dropped out of school, and whose parents had no money to send their son to college. No one in our family had been to college before. There was nothing to model after. I was a kid, without a workable plan, only a destination, and no way to get there. Then I realized that there are no more powerful tools than belief and faith. They allow us to see what's not seen. They enable us to imagine what seems unimaginable and it can sustain you, even when reality tells you that you are starving. I believed that I was going to college, but I had no idea how to get there.

My father wanted me to get a job working for the city. For a Black man, that meant becoming a security guard, working all your life, and ending up with retirement packages. If I didn't want to do that, he suggested I join the military and make a career out of it. We fought often. If he said to go right, I most definitely was going left. I hate to use a football analogy, but it is fitting. You need to score, but the first thing you must do is the training to get into the game. Life had become my training ground and I was the student. Next, when you get the ball, your goal is to move forward. You may have some setbacks, but the goal is to fight, scratch, and do whatever you need to go forward. The world, people, and Satan will try to stop you; however, you must become a warrior. I had the fuel needed to make a change. I wanted to prove to everyone that I was not stupid or a loser. I continued to work out and told anyone who would listen that I was going to college. The plan was to go to a junior college, then transfer to the University of Texas. I would kill two birds with one stone. I would make my parents proud by being the local kid who came back home and did well.

I remember as a kid going to church with my parents, the pastor mentioned that a University of Texas player's parents was in the audience. It didn't matter that he was not there. His parents were there, and the pastor asked them to stand. They stood and everyone clapped. They received a place of honor that I wanted my parents to have. Deep down I wanted them to be proud of me. I wanted them to receive their place of honor. That was my goal, but a vision without a plan is just a dream. I can't say I was faithfully praying all the time. After hearing from God, I stopped praying with the same desperate need. My relationship with the Almighty was like my relationship with the world: I kept to myself and only spoke when needed. It's a good thing that's not how God works. He had a plan for me. One day in the gym, I met a guy named Joe

Martin. I won't mention names a lot in this book, but this one is important. Joe gave me a chance. God does work in mysterious ways, and very often people have no idea that they are being used by Him. Joe Martin was a pretty wild guy. He was so wild, that twenty-five years later he called me to apologize about his behavior during that period of my life.

That took a lot of courage, and I respected him for it. But at the time, he was a wild man; fast-talking, big-dreaming, and wanting to become an agent. When we met, his comment was, "How old are you? Man, you are way too big to be doing nothing." He told me about a junior college in Oakland, California, and that he may be able to speak to them about me playing football. It was amazing to see what was happening, and how God was working. I saw the blessing, but I also covered it with fear. Fear had always been a factor in my life, but now it was right in my face. I had never been outside of Austin, except in fifth grade, when we went to Dallas to Six Flags. I had never been on a plane. I had never been anywhere farther than walking distance from my home and school.

Sometimes we don't see how blessed we are because our minds are clouded with junk. I was afraid of the unknown. I also concluded that if I stayed in Austin, it would be too easy for me to fail. It would be too easy to make an excuse as to why I didn't make it and go back to the life I had. So, I took a chance. In retrospect, most successful people take risks. I decided to go to California and become a football player. I had my idea of how things would work out. I would go to school out of town, play so well that the University of Texas would say they wanted one of their own back. I would become a local hero, and my parents would be announced at church. They would stand up with pride when the pastor mentioned my name. That was my plan, and so I no longer had a dream, I was the dream. I don't think anyone believed that I was going; in fact, no one had ever heard of the junior college in Oakland. Heck, no one knew where Oakland was. Joe told me there were no guarantees I would make the team and that I would have to pay my own way. They didn't offer scholarships, but it was a chance, and a chance I was willing to take it. I was ready to leave. There were too many old habits back home. Sometimes we must leave the fertile field of bad habits to go and be replanted on new ground. I had to do something different.

Everything was set but then came the hard part. I had to get ready for my trip. I had to train, I had to be ready, because I was adamant that I would not fail or quit or be a loser. I hated those words, and it was not going to describe me. I didn't party much, but I had to get rid of the things that would hold me back. I would forsake the things that would hinder me and push into the things that would give me life. And so I trained. I continued to lift weights but did it with more passion. I went from benching 300 pounds to 400 pounds. I also ran with intent. We lived next to a school that had an outdoor basketball court. I did my running at night. The same basketball court and park that I use to play at became my training ground. The little sand area that held the swings and seesaws became my obstacle course, the street sidewalk was my track, and the night was my cover. I remember running and saying to myself, "I am the best, will be the best, have to be the best, nothing will stop me. I will not quit again." I pushed my body, harder than any coach could. When it was time to perform, I would be ready. I did box jumps on a concrete wall, sprints up and down the sidewalk. I ran until I wanted to give up, and then I would run some more. Everyone thought I was crazy, but I had a plan, a vision, and faith that it was going to come true. I was fueled by anger, by the desire to prove everyone wrong, to prove that I was not some stupid kid. I was on fire. Yet, whoever heard of Laney Junior College? Was that even a school? In Oakland, California? It was so far away and into the unknown, but sometimes in life, you have to take a chance. Joe was in my ear encouraging me to keep going. He even helped me get a job at a lumber company, and even there I practiced. I worked two jobs and trained. I had no time for anything else, but that was okay. I did not have anything else.

The dream was coming true, and it was time to make the move. I wanted to argue with my parents the day I left. I wanted to throw my hands in the air and tell them to take a hike. I wanted it to imitate the karate movies where the hero would leave angry and come back a master, but it never happened that way. Instead, my parents were sad to see their son go. My mom said with tears in her eyes, "Why do you have to go so far?" It was not what I wanted. It would have been a lot easier if they were mad, but I was still thinking like a child. They did love me, but sometimes you must do what you have to do. My life had been molded by TV shows and I lived my life like episodes. There were not supposed to be real feelings involved. I tucked it away and compartmentalized how I felt. I pushed it down. I was emotionless, as I had trained myself: "Don't feel the pain; control." I guess that's why I always identified with Spock, from the original *Star Trek*. There was the human side of me, but I had pushed it down for the Vulcan side to win. My parents had no money to give me. They had nothing to send off their child with other than their love.

6

The Journey

I don't remember getting on the plane or the trip. It probably seems like something I should look on with fond memories, but I don't. It was just another task, another step toward my goal, and something that could be easily forgotten. I do remember my dad and me at the airport trying to hug to say goodbye. It was something we'd never done before. Don't get me wrong, I have no doubt that my dad loved me, but he grew up in a time where expressing emotions could get you hanged. A good Black man in Texas had to be the strong, silent type. He had to work hard, get a stable job with security, and not cause too many problems. He had to be strong to his own family, but not so strong in the world to cause problems. My dad never caused many problems, but he wasn't a pushover; when need be, he was a lion. One of the proudest moments I had as a child happened one day when I was walking with my dad and brothers and some cowards drove by in a pickup truck and yelled out the word, "Niggers." I was young at the time but knew it was hate. I thought to myself, "Why? You don't know us. You don't know where we come from. You know nothing about us, so why would you yell out hate?" I blinked and my dad was off running after the truck. He wouldn't allow them or anyone else to put us down and my dad could run. They used to call him "the horse" when he was in school running track because he had a smooth gallop like a horse and was fast. He was closing in on the truck until they were able to speed away. He was a man and would fight to the death for his family. He and my mom sacrificed so much for us.

At the airport, the strong silent type (my dad) looked at me. I had seen this scene before on TV and was now living it. There would be a pause, a moment of silence, and then the two men would embrace in tears. We looked at each other for an awkward moment not sure what to say. "Be safe, son. Call us if you need us," he spoke. My head was down as I nodded. We made a move toward each other knowing it was what we were supposed to do, but not sure what the next steps were. My dad reached out to hug me, but I put my wall up giving a half hug. I gave him the "men don't do that and I'm not going to let you get too close to me vibe," so we said goodbye and that was it. I was off to the great unknown and walking into my destiny.

I traveled with another young man named Vernon Hadnot. He, too, was walking in his dream. He was a good player who happened to not get picked up by a college. I think being young, good-looking, and partying too much caught up with him, so he had to take a step back and go to a junior college to move up to the next level. We were both taking a journey set in motion by Joe Martin. Laney Junior College had never gotten players from out of town before, so we would be their great experiment. I sat wide-eyed on the plane marveling at how it took off and how we were floating in the air. I was like a kid in a candy store. There was no fear—excitement took over. I think I made some small talk with Vernon but was just trying to enjoy the moment. He was a talker and always had a bright smile and sunny attitude, which was a good trait, but not for me.

When we finally arrived in Oakland, the head coach, Stan Peters was there to pick us up. I laugh now because seeing him for the first time was not what I was expecting. He was a short white guy with one motto, "Go." He looked at us, and I am sure he was wondering what in the world was he doing taking kids from Texas. He must have believed this was a great waste of time, but since Joe had coached there before, he would give it a try. I tried to look cool. I had gotten a Jheri curl before I left and was trying to be trendy. I probably looked like a fool, but in my mind I was cool. The curl did not fully take, so some of my hair was straight, some curly, some nappy.

We walked, struggling to keep up with the coach as he was a man about action, movement, and go. I looked at Vernon and could tell he was thinking the same thing. Pete looked old to us, yet he walked like his life depended on it. Thinking back, a white coach in a mostly Black school and neighborhood, I probably would walk fast also. His famous line was, "Life is really simple. Do well, work hard, and, if you did not like it, it was either my way or the highway." It was understood, and he was the boss. The plan was to stay at a relative of Vernon's for a bit until we could find our own place. Laney could not pay for anything, and they made that clear, but they would help us find a spot.

We were dropped off at Vernon's relative and by my standards the guy was rich. I think he had a three-bedroom place that he lived in by himself. Seeing a man with that much house was amazing. For my family, it was three bedrooms growing up for nine people. We stayed there until we found an apartment. This was a mission, and the doors of heaven were flying open.

The time to put up or shut up came and it was time to start training. I was amazed at how fast Vernon was and how he seemed to run as if he floated on air. I could run but had no training other than what I taught myself. My running was based on power and determination. Vernon seemed to run as if lifted by angels. It was decided that I was going to be a linebacker. The reason was that all I had to do was just hit someone and I had been doing that all my life. The training became intense, but it was something I could handle. I had pushed my body hard enough so when the coaches tried to push me there was no comparison. We practiced in the middle of downtown Oakland. My teammates were drug dealers, dropouts, and people working three jobs for a chance to go somewhere. We were all dreamers. I did look good on paper. I had the height, weight, and strength to play football, but it had almost been two years since I put on any pads, and I'm sure I looked a mess. I played linebacker—Hulk hit, Hulk smash—which was the perfect fit for me. The only difference between TV and real life was that players hit back, and when they do, it hurt. I had made up my mind to feel no pain and be the one giving pain.

Vernon and I were having an adjustment period. I think it was the first time the both of us had been on our own, so we both brought our own baggage with us. Vernon was an only child and his family had some money. I was one of seven and had no money, except for the wad of money from working that I had been saving for rent. Being on my own for the first time and having cash is not the best combo. I don't think we did anything foolish with our money, but I found myself running out of money quickly and by the looks of things, I would be a poor man struggling to get by.

The first couple of weeks, Vernon and I got along. He had his food, I had mine, and as long as things were separate, we were good. Life is always good when things go the way you want them to, but struggles define your character. The first few months Vernon's family would send him money, boxes of groceries, and whatever else he needed. When I ran out and only had enough for rent, I struggled. Vernon, being an only child, did what he knew to do, which was to take care of himself. My thought in life was that we should all take care of each other. In hindsight, we both saw things differently. There was no right or wrong way, just different. I was trying to mooch off him and he was trying to survive by keeping what he had. It's understandable from both sides, and depending on who is writing the book, both ways made sense. I hate to say that there was a time when I took (stole) some of his food because I had none. It was wrong and I felt sorry for doing it, but I was starving and in desperate need. I would send letters to my family about needing money to survive and waiting every day at the mailbox for something. They would try, but it took a long time. I imagine they were waiting for payday. When the money came, it was not much. Imagine trying to play football, working out like a madman, and asking your parents for money. You wait at the mailbox for a week, then two weeks, then three, and nothing has come. The fourth week you get a letter. You think that you will eat like a king because all your prayers have been answered. You open the letter and out pops a crisp five-dollar bill. I was mad. I wanted money and this was what I got. *"But he said to me, "My grace is sufficient for you, for my power is made perfect in weakness." Therefore I will boast all the more gladly about my weaknesses, so that Christ's power may rest on me. That is why, for Christ's sake, I delight in weaknesses, in insults, in hardships, in persecutions, in difficulties. For when I am weak, then I am strong."* (2 Corinthians 12:9-10)

7

Faith

Things had now gotten worse in terms of food; I would buy a box of pancake mix and use it for my breakfast, lunch, and dinner. It was not a good recipe for putting on muscle, but I managed and kept going. You may ask, "Where was God in all this?" It's a good question because He was there even when I did not speak to Him. I didn't understand about fellowshipping, I was still a loner. I attended church out there once or twice and I did make a vow that I would glorify His name, but that was in the past and I was dealing with the present. I did read the Bible from front to back, but without teaching. I was just reading.

The benefit of having a roommate who played on the opposing team was that you didn't have to fight with him at home. Vernon was good, but I was angry and hungry, and I tried to knock his head off during practice. I blamed him, and he was going to pay for my pain. I thanked God for good coaches, and once I had my sights set on someone, I took care of business. I was like a hate-seeking missile. Even with all of that, over time Vernon and I became friends. We were like brothers on a journey together. We were the first two guys they ever tried to get from out of town and at the end of the day, we only had each other to depend on.

I know I was a jerk at times. I once got a huge rubber snake and put it in his bed because I knew he was afraid of snakes. I knew he'd pull back his covers and hopefully see it and jump. Because we slept in the same room, I sat and waited. When the moment came, he made an unexpected move. He turned off the lights and jumped into bed. The next thing I heard was a scream. He jumped out of bed, furious. Vernon swung the closest thing to him at me, and I pretended to be innocent. I looked at him in disbelief. He was trying to kill me with a broom. I started to laugh in the middle of his rage. I couldn't help it. I was bigger, stronger, meaner, and faster, and he was going to kill me with a broom. I couldn't control my laugher. After a minute we calmed down and both started to laugh. There are so many stupid ways that friendships are born.

That first year at Laney was tough, not just with practice, but living was tough. But with faith, I persevered. There were days I felt like quitting, but when you are part of a family and you see that they are going through the same things you are going through, it is hard to let your teammates down. I also did not want to go back home a failure. I wanted to be a winner and not a loser. I understand that leadership has less to do with size and more to do with what is in the heart. Several guys set a good example. Laney was viewed as a last-ditch effort by many of the guys. Rasco was one of those guys whom I knew would never make it to the pros, but he believed he could. He worked three jobs, went to school, and played football. He slept three to four hours per night. This was his only chance, and he was going to take it.

There was this one time, after my workout and with not enough water in my system, I found myself at the bottom of the hill that led to our apartment. I learned a long time ago when I used to walk several miles to work to take things one step at a time. Set small goals with the big picture in mind. I decided to turn my walk home into a training exercise. Instead of walking this hill, I ran it, even though my body screamed out for rest and water. I made it to the top and then felt a cramp in my right arm. It was painful and I tried to try to rub it out with my other arm. The other arm locked up on me and then both my legs. I don't know if you have ever had a cramp so bad that your whole body locks up, but I couldn't move, and we lived on the second floor of an apartment building. I was in the fetal position at the bottom of the stairs leading up to our apartment. A few people saw me, but instead of asking if I needed any help, they just watched. That was the culture around those parts: don't get involved or you could become a target as well. They must have thought I was on drugs or something. This was a full-body cramp and could have been very dangerous. I was locked up and needed to get out of the sun and get some fluids in my body. I crawled on all fours painfully up the stairs, forcing my mind to push my body beyond the pain. I made it to the top and couldn't get the keys in because my hands had cramped up as well. I pushed my mind past the pain and managed to get the door open, but my body was frozen. I lay on my back like a dead roach, arm and legs grossly curled up in the air. I couldn't just stay there and allow them to look and laugh at me, so I willed myself to push my body in the house. I closed the door and lay there for a while until my body was finally released. That was the life of a player who wanted it.

We lived in Oakland and had guys on the team who were drug dealers, but if you knew their story, they weren't all bad guys. Yes, they sold drugs, but for them, it was their only way of survival. One guy, a big guy who played on the defense, was nice, but also a drug dealer. He would leave a wad of money on the bench at times forgetting to put it away. Everyone knew it was his money and it was not to be touched. There were hundreds of dollars just lying there. Take it and you could lose your life. We had a deaf player along with others from the Somalia-Pacific Islands. They had all the natural talent but came from a culture where things were much laid back; they didn't see the need to work hard. One guy name Maca could walk in off the street and bench press 400 pounds easily, but his goal in life was to sing, have fun and relax. Having visited some of the islands later in my life, I now understood their point of view.

My life had been focused and hard work up until this point, but I had also been injured frequently during my first year. I had weak ankles and nearly half the season I would sprain them or do something to set me back; the difference was that I would not let it stop me. I'd put some tape on it and keep going. I had so much tape on my ankles that I could only walk straight ahead because I couldn't move it in any other direction. I planned to charge full force ahead. The head coach, Coach Peters, or Pete as we called him, was a no-nonsense guy. He made us work hard, laid down the law, and told us how he wanted us to go out of Laney and into a four-year school so he told us some of the successes he had and some of the failures; some of the great talents that couldn't make it to the next level because they grew up with one foot in the street and the other foot on the field.

Pete also made sure that every one of his athletes would take a speech class. The class was taught by an African

American teacher, and it was a great feeling to know that one of us could be that good of a speaker. I'm not trying to sound racist, but at that time there were very few African American sports commentators. I think OJ Simpson was the only one, so having someone teach us how to speak was a good thing. I learned a lot from some of these classes and our coach. People now think I'm natural at certain things, but I had a good teacher. You see, when you are quiet and insecure, there is a sense that people are laughing at you. That gets added to your arsenal when you play football. Eventually, those who were smart knew they had to be careful with me. It was the street mentality.

My love life was more of my self-life. I didn't care how they looked; I was just happy they wanted me. Whether they were blind, crippled, or crazy, as long as they wanted me, I was good to go. That's the problem with many young men: low self-esteem or over self-esteem, both of which can be dangerous. I was a big guy, so I had a few ladies, but not a lot. Oakland was hardcore and my game was bad. Girls would roll their eyes as I tried to say something that normally came out corny. When they did give me their attention I would sink more into my shell and not pick up on the signals. I didn't know anything about relationships, other than sex. It was strange, but during my first year, two women hung around me all the time. It seems as though they were my bodyguards and they looked good. I'm not sure what their game was, but they were always on my side. It was never about sex. Maybe they saw potential and I was status or arm candy. I didn't complain, yet it was kind of weird. Lucky for me, God was looking out. He sent me Janice, my girlfriend then and now my wife.

With a girlfriend comes the need for money. There was a time I was so desperate for money that I thought about becoming a model. There were ads in the newspapers of people looking for male models. I responded to one of these ads. I saw a gentleman sitting behind a desk. He looked at me and asked me to take off my shirt. I should have thought something fishy, but I was desperate for money and was proud of my body. Of course, this was outside of God's plan, but I was going to do it on my own. I took my shirt off and he said, "Great. What we are looking for is someone to do a workout video at a park." He told me a couple of areas I could work on to get my body in perfect shape but said I could get the job. I was excited. I wanted to show everyone that I had made it. I asked him where the video would be shown and he said, "I'm going, to be honest with you. Our videos are for the gay porn industry and that is more than likely where we would have your video." I almost fainted. I told him no thanks. Be who you are, but that was not me.

My linebacker coach was a Japanese American guy named Jay Uchiumi, whom I stared at for several minutes the first time I met him. I had never seen a Japanese football player or coach before, so I was amazed. I thought he was the coolest guy around because he was funny and would tell us a joke before practice began. One of the great things about sports is that it allows you to see life outside of the box and meet people from other races with whom you might not normally interact. The fact that Jay knew football blew my mind. I know I must have frustrated him to death because I was this big kid who knew very little about football, nothing about how to drop into coverage, nothing about how to pass rush or cover a tight end. I was so raw that at times he would shake his head and just say go get the quarterback.

My life's patterns had revealed themselves once again. I was a good student in school but relied heavily on my natural ability both on the football field and in school instead of study habits. I had a counselor Milton Shimabukuro, but we called him Milt. His family liked us. My parents, TV, and God made for a polite, young man and so I think they were surprised how I handled myself. There were days that I was starving, and Milt and his family saved my butt. They would cook for me and Vernon as if they were cooking for ten people. Milt would also find odd jobs for me to do around his house so that I could make some money. I could handle just about any physical work, and I would just keep going until they said stop. I had no complaints, no attitude, just a grateful young man, happy that someone cared enough to help. All the coaches became my friend and helped us as much as they legally could.

They were family, and they looked out for us. Milt would guide me as far as grades and classes. Pete, Uch, Ole, and Coach Martinez took care of us on the field. I'm sure there are others I've forgotten. It's not because they didn't help me on my journey, but because there are so many and I have trouble remembering names, so please forgive me for not mentioning your name.

The one lasting memory I have as a player was Coach Martinez running us after practice. I'll remember this story until the day I die. We were having fun and not taking practice seriously enough, and I believe he snapped. He gathered us all together, so we thought the practice was over. He looked at us and calmly said "Have you ever heard of Dr. Jekyll and Mr. Hyde?" We all looked at him like he was crazy. He yelled, "Well, I am Mr. Hyde, now start running." I've never run so hard in my life. I would have walked off the field if it hadn't been for a guy named Chris Parnell. Chris was a linebacker who played despite his small stature and would take anyone. He encouraged me, as well as everyone else, to keep going. On that day, he was the leader, and I was the teammate.

The first season was my chance to start living out my destiny. I wasn't the best student of the game, but my size, speed, strength, and desire made up for a lot of my mistakes. I was now a linebacker, but my technique was poor, so I made a lot of my plays through hard work and heart. I always believed there were three types of players. If you master one of the three, you can go far. If you master two of them, you can develop a name for yourself and maybe go to the pro bowl. If you master all three, you become a megastar, the type of player that transcends teams. The three categories of player are as follow:

1)   YOU ARE A NATURAL ATHLETE

There are a lot of good athletes, but some stand above the rest. If you find a way to maximize your natural ability so you stand out freakishly above everyone else, you have a good shot at making it very far.

2)   YOU PLAY WITH A LOT OF HEART

Some players will do whatever it takes to get the job done. If the coach says to run a mile, you run two miles. If he tells you to play a different position, you master that position. You are willing to do whatever you have to get the job done. This is usually in combination with another skill set, but it is the heart. When you see someone running downfield and everyone thinks it is a lost cause, you still try.

3)   YOU ARE A GREAT STUDENT, WHO HAS MASTERED STUDYING THE GAME

You know it so well that people think you are cheating. You seem to know where the play is going, even before the other team does. You can adjust on the fly because, as a good student, you have weighted all possibilities and how to react to them.

If you master any one of these, you will surely stand out. If you can get all of them, you become a stud. I mastered two of them: I worked harder than anyone and I pushed myself to become a great athlete. I did not study as much as I should have and so the transition was not always easy. I played well enough to get some attention and my natural athletic abilities and hard work allowed me to soar. I was still the quiet kid who tried to please, so I was ideal in terms of setting a good example as a good person. My parents also laid a good foundation. I was becoming what I saw.

My best friend at Laney was Charles Gatson. We worked out all the time, and like most introverts, you find one friend and you stick with them. Charles was that person for me, the person I trusted the most. The gym had beat-up weights, some mirrors, and large paintings of bodybuilders on the wall. I used to look at each of those pictures and envision myself as one of them. You can always become what you see if you look at it long enough and are willing to work to make it happen. I was becoming the comic book characters that I read all the time. I'm convinced that belief is one of the greatest tools to push you beyond what you think you can do, but it can also work in reverse. If you believe a negative, it can push you into believing and even moving toward your belief. Think of Michael Jackson and his nose and how his brother's made fun of him, which led to all the plastic surgeries. Some people look good, but their quest for perfection is never satisfied. That is how I felt about my chest.

I had worked out and pushed my body into something that I was proud of. It was something that gave me a sense of being, yet before I went away to college, I had a scar on my chest. It was a couple of keloids. My body was my temple, my prize, and I had two small keloids on it. I freaked out and made this situation worse by trying to treat myself. By the time I got to college, I had two marks on my chest. I would not take off my shirt in my first year. I was afraid of what people would think. We often see things as worse than they are when the reality is that it is often not as bad as we think. We have to learn to disregard junk thoughts. I was not there yet, and it took a conversation with my best friend Charles to get me beyond my insecurity. We were in the locker room after practice at a school in the heart of downtown Oakland. We didn't have to shower in the locker rooms, so I never took my shirt off in front of anyone. If I did, I'd find a way to do it quickly. Charles then asks about my scar on this occasion. The conversation went something like this:

"Man, what is wrong with you, it can't be that big," Charles said in response to my reluctance to take off my shirt.

"Man, it's big."

"Come on, man, show me."

"Naw, it's huge."

Charles sighed, "You going to show me or not?"

"Okay, but you got to promise not to stare at it."

"Okay, I promise."

I took my shirt off for the first time around someone. Charles is staring at my chest for a moment, and then says, "Man, it's not that big."

"Really?"

"Yea, I thought it was going to be bigger."

Now, I want you to imagine that you just happened to be walking by the locker room and you heard that conversation between two muscular men. Sometimes you have to laugh at being an idiot and thank God for friends who help you break outside of your comfort zone.

8

God's Plan

My first year playing football after taking two years off was pretty good. I think the coaches were happy with the guys they got from Texas. We represented ourselves well. This was our chance to do something right, and I think Joe Martin was smart enough to recommend two young men that had the right attitude for the task. We saw ourselves as representatives for Texas. Being a representative is enough to keep you on track. Remember the Bible says we are representatives or ambassadors of Christ. That is who we were, even though no one in Texas knew us. Our families knew us, and we took on that responsibility. If you work hard in the beginning, you will see the fruit later in life. Such is the case with our journey as football players. After the first year, I had developed a name for myself. I was strong, powerful, and by junior college standards, I was a good player. I wasn't the best, but I played well enough to gain respect. My reputation was that I never stopped going. Maybe because I was messing up on plays and had to make up for it somehow, or the fact that through my hardships, God had used that as a training ground, but whatever the case, I kept going. For example, we had a game, but I had not eaten a good meal in a while and was out of cash. I needed energy so I donated blood to get some money. This was in the eighties, so I figured I could guzzle down some raw eggs and milk to get a quick boost of energy, just like in the movie *Rocky*. I played the game, but half of what I swallowed came back up. I still managed to finish the game.

My second year was much better. The coaches liked me and tried to help me find summer work. I was able to earn enough money to support myself without relying on my parents. Milt, Uch, and Pete saw me as more than just a piece of meat and felt it was their responsibility to assist us in any way they could without breaking any rules. They assisted me in applying for grants, finding employment, and treating me as if I were a son. It was pretty cool. On the other hand, Vernon's family stopped sending him as much food, and the flow of money slowed. The situation was reversed, but we were family and helped each other out. There were no hard feelings on either side. We just needed to survive, and the year coming up was going to allow us to go to a four-year college.

My love life had also changed. A young lady named Janice was a cheerleader for the team. If you think the players were a mixture of whatever, so were the cheerleaders. The cheerleader tryouts can be summed up like this: there was an eighty-year-old lady who tried out and almost made the squad. I think we had some strippers. We had some ladies who should not have been in a short outfit, and some who knew nothing about football. Janice was from England. Her knowledge of football was limited, and each cheerleader had a tagline. Janice's name was "English Toffee." She still had a bit of a British accent and I thought she was the sexiest one there. She had been in the Navy before coming to Oakland and had the body of a fitness goddess. She wasn't overly muscular, but she had the perfect proportion of curves. In my first year, I had been eyeballing her. I noticed she was different from the other girls. (Remember, I had no money at the time, only two pairs of pants and three shirts, so I did not think she would want to talk to me.) The girls on campus seemed to be interested in guys who seemed to have something going for them. Success is all relative. You were prime if you had a car, or something that suggested you had money at the time. Janice was not that type of person. I don't think she cared at all about what a person had, and she was not the type to go with the crowd. She did hang out with her friends but would just as quickly turn down a party or anything else. I think at one time MC Hammer tried to get at her, and she turned him away.

In our first year at Laney College, we did not like each other. I thought she was just like everyone else. She had several small gold chains on her neck and all the guys were trying to get with her. I thought she was too good for me and that was a big turnoff. I also did not like the fact that in one game when we were on defense, they started cheering for the offense to go. They had not been watching the game and these were our cheerleaders. On the flip side, she thought I was egotistic and just like every other jock. I had the two girls on my arm all the time, so she thought I was a player of women. We were both wrong about each other; however, during our second year we connected.

I had a job at the school doing campus security. I was a rent-a-cop. I had no gun, no badge, just a bright yellow shirt to yell out for help if there was ever any trouble. I took my job seriously and Charles worked the job also. We would walk from one end of the campus to the other looking out for trouble and making sure things were safe. My TV world was coming to life. I was a superhero. As fate would have it, Janice walked home from school late one night when I was working. The school had a long, dimly lit underpass that you could take as a shortcut to the street. If it was a house, it would be a basement that led to the street. All kinds of people walked there, and you never knew if someone high on drugs, or crazy might take the shortcut along the way also. There was always a smell of pee. It was dark and there were areas where you could do your business without anyone seeing you. Janice was walking home one night, and I was on duty. She said I scared her to death when I came out of nowhere and told her that she should not be walking alone at night by herself. It was one of those situations where you are not supposed to be doing something, but for the sake of time, you do it anyhow and hope for the best. I happened to be watching the whole thing and, deep in my heart, I was concerned about her being alone late at night and walking through the underpass though I knew nothing was going to happen to her while I was on duty. I walked up to her as any Texas gentleman would, and I told her I would walk her across that area to make sure she was safe. I'm sure she thought I was going to murder her and dump her body somewhere, but she agreed. I walked her to the edge of the school in my bright yellow jacket. I was doing what I was supposed to do, and even if it did not lead to anything, I knew I was doing what was right. We both made it to the edge of the campus, and I asked where she was going. She said she was walking home. Some parts of Oakland are not the safest place. I had seen girls getting cussed out because they did not give up their phone numbers. There were drug dealers, pimps, and hookers on the corners. I could not let her walk the rest of the way home alone. It would not be right. What would Superman do? What would the Hulk do? What would Thor or the Six-Million-Dollar man do? I told her I would walk her home.

A pretty face can make you do some great and some stupid things. I think this was somewhere in between. I took off my jacket and got on my little walkie-talkie and told Charles I would be back in a little bit. It was a stupid idea to leave the campus. Anything could have happened. Charles could have been jumped, someone else could have been harmed, yet in my mind, I was doing the right thing. I walked Janice home and that was the beginning of our relationship. We both found out how special the other person was. What we initially thought of each other was wrong. She was a great, humble, beautiful person. I could not believe my luck. I had this very beautiful woman speaking to me. My comic book world was coming to life. I made a point to walk her home as many nights as she had classes. We eventually became known as Pebbles and Bam Bam.

We had a lot in common, and I was in love. Our grades were usually posted outside the classrooms. I told her late one night, while I was on duty, that I wanted to check on my grades. We were alone and I got my first kiss from her. Love was in the air. God provided for me above and beyond what I thought I deserved.

Janice often tells the story of me getting mad and pulling a tree out of the ground. It wasn't a tree, but it was one of those large wooden pegs used to hold the tree up and we were having an argument. I was mad and Janice was good at dismissing me. Like the Hulk, it was enough to enrage me, so I don't know for what reason, but I pulled this large piece of wood out of the ground. There was dirt and grass still hanging from it when I yelled for Janice to come back and talk to me. Janice would not even look at me. The other players on the team thought I was crazy. For the record, I was not going to do anything with the tree. I'm not sure why I pulled it out. I had learned a long time ago to take my anger out on inanimate objects, like weights or trees, instead of people. Janice eventually came to me, and we talked. I had moved places and situations, but I still had me to deal with.

I lived my life subliminally, just like TV shows. When I was growing up, there were shows on tv where things would be going one way and then some dramatic event would happen, and then things would change. I guess that is what I thought would happen in real life and in some ways it did. Janice is smart, very efficient, and very organized. She was a very structured person, thanks to her British background. She dressed well, her clothes well-matched and organized. She had about five very thin gold chains on her neck that she worked hard to purchase. After leaving the Navy, she lived with a young lady she met while in the military. Her friend Missy was like a sister that she never had, and Missy's mom Connie took her in. There was a strength about Janice that allowed her to push through every circumstance. She had that something about her that brought beauty to every situation. While I dare say that she was not perfect, she was perfect for me.

We worked together during my offseason at the naval supply center, which was a big storage building. When orders came in, we would go to the different locations within the building and get the supplies. It was a simple job but one that we could do together. We sometimes passed love notes to each other in the bins we were using to collect supplies. God had a plan for us. People we never met before would come up to us and say those very words. They prophesied that God had something in store for us. They would say there was something special about us. I remember one bus driver, a big brother, who had huge arms like a bodybuilder, treated us with respect like we were adults. The culture of some people back then was a prison mentality. They would smile in your face but the moment you weren't around, they would try to get your girl. He seemed to have everything going for him, but he never tried and showed nothing but respect. He was a good example that there were still good people looking out for us. Some bus drivers would see us running in the rain to catch the bus and because we were not at the bus stop, they would keep going. They would go fast enough so we could not catch them, but slow enough that we saw the people in the back of the bus laughing at us. At least we got into shape.

I played my last year of football at Laney and did very well. I wasn't known in Texas, but I had built a reputation at Laney. My greatest desire was for the University of Texas to come knocking on the door and ask me to come back, but it never happened. It would have been a dream to play for UT; to come back as a hero. It would have been my movie that became a reality, but sometimes our plans are not God's plans; *For I know the plans that I have for you,' declares the LORD, 'plans for welfare and not for calamity to give you a future and a hope* (Jeremiah 29:11).

By the end of the year, I received letters from several schools that expressed an interest in giving me a scholarship: Michigan, Michigan State, USC, UCLA, Cal Berkeley, and others. I couldn't believe it. This was my moment to prove to my old coach, my family, the people who knew me, that I was not stupid, that I was not going to be a loser all my life. The coaches asked me where I wanted to go. The prevailing wisdom at the time was not to decide based on a girlfriend but to do what was best for my career. Love would follow if it was meant to be. I chose Cal, but I know that God had His guiding hand over me. The promise that He made, that I had a destiny and a purpose, was coming to the light. This was my thought process in choosing Cal. If I went to the University of California, I would be next to my girlfriend Janice, and it would be a big middle finger to everyone who thought I was not going to make it. I would have a better chance of making it to the pros since there was a guy named Hardy Nickerson who was playing linebacker at the time, and he would be a senior. I knew if the scouts were coming there to watch him, they would have to watch me. Hardy was inside linebacker and I was outside linebacker. I had taken my step of faith and was ready to take another one. Normally, this would be where I would say that I got on my hands and knees and asked God for directions, but I had stopped asking God. I had stopped seeking God. I was just living in the now and had forgotten my relationship with Him. But just like a friend you have not seen for years, God was still there and we were still friends. We just hadn't seen each other in a while.

I was able to take a recruiting trip to Cal Berkley and I told them I did not want the superstars taking me around and showing me all the good stuff. I wanted one of the non-superstar guys to show me around. That way I could get a real feel, an inside scoop, on what the school was really like. It was flawed thinking. Whomever they got was still going to give the best report about the school, but I thought I would be able to tell what was going on. I remember going to the campus and although it wasn't that far away from Laney, it might as well have been in another country for me. It was beautiful, with rolling hills, and beautiful people. It was golden. It was a

complete change for me, but to top it off, it was a smart school.
I wasn't worried about how smart a school it was, and maybe
I should have, but one thing about being an athlete is you can
fool yourself into being overly confident in things that you
shouldn't be. I figured I was pretty smart. I did okay at Laney,
and to me, okay was similar to brilliant, so I was good to go.

I met a guy named Sydney Johnson at Cal who showed
me around. The funny turn of events was that he was in
Virginia when I was playing for the Redskins. He said they
tested most of the recruits without us knowing about it. They
would take us to play a simple game of basketball, to see what
we had as far as being an athlete. I could not shoot hoops that
well, but I knew what I could do. I did a 360° dunk from
standing under the goal. No stutter step, no running start, just
bend my legs, 360°, and dunk. They were impressed. Sydney
gave a good report and they wanted me on their team. When
it came time to make the decision, I picked Cal.

I remember hearing stories on the news about how
players were getting paid under the table and making a killing.
I thought this happened at all schools. I could not have been
more wrong. The day I made my announcement we had
someone there taking pictures. It was a big deal, "A local guy
from Laney Junior College going to Cal." This was the first
time something like this happened. The guy from Cal came in

and gave me a Cal sweatshirt and cap to take pictures so I thought I was now on easy street. After the picture, he took everything back. They could not give me anything; those were the rules. I still had two pairs of pants and three shirts. I had my girl, I had the school, and I had a team.

Joe Kapp was the coach, and he was a wild guy. He had that "anything was possible" look and he would demonstrate it every day before they fired him. I came in being what I thought was a freak of nature only to realize that everyone there was a freak of nature. On the field, I had my challenges. Despite my speed and quickness, I had a hard time covering someone and getting to the ball. I also couldn't catch it. As they say, "I couldn't catch a cold butt naked in Alaska." Their only choice was to have me as a pass rusher. This created some benefits and some problems. In practice, they would have the linebackers go one-on-one against the running back in a pass-rush drill. The drill was meant to teach the running backs how to block a blitzing linebacker. It was unfair to the running backs, but if they were good and learned, they would have a good base and take on anyone in the open field. Don Nobles, one of my best friends, now laughs at how he would watch the young rookies go up against me and how I would destroy them. It was pretty simple in my mind: get into their heads with my strength and then kill them with my speed. The first guy lined up against me and I hit him like he stole something. The next guy was already freaking out because of what I did to the first guy, so I used some speed on him. They weren't big bruisers. These were super smart guys, with really high GPAs who happened to play football. Some of them were even walk-ons who just loved the game. After beating a bunch of the guys, they all moved out of the way to let Don Nobles take care of me. We were roughly the same size, and he could hit. He was a Black guy in a predominantly all-white school, and I was another Black kid coming in. He had been with the school for several years and I was the new guy. He was going to show me how to play ball the Cal way. Don stood ready. I stood ready. The coaches gathered around.

The whistle blew and the two bulls collided. We clashed like thunder, but I recovered quicker, so I won. Coaches have their pride, and the linebacker coach was yelling and jumping up and down. The running back coach was pissed. "Do it again," he shouted. Players gathered around. Everyone waited and practice was halted. Bull versus bull. I felt the last hit Don put on me and it hurt, yet he would never, ever know. We hit again, but I got him with strength and speed. We did this about four or five times. I won them all, although I felt cross-eyed after it was over. After practice, I came up to Don and told him good job. I told him I felt every one of his hits. He looked at me like I was kidding. He was still shaking his head trying to overcome the effects. I did not talk much, so saying anything to him was stepping out of my comfort zone. He had my respect because I knew that we either had to be friends or we would end up killing each other. That was the beginning of our friendship, and we are still friends, thirty years later.

Football is a great game. I don't care what anyone says; it is a great way to learn teamwork and to learn about people. You are fighting for something together, trying to be the best at whatever you are doing. You learn to rely on the person right next to you. I had never been around so many white people in my life, but football taught me to judge each person based on who they were, not the color of their skin. Of course, there will always be idiots from every race. We had some guys on the O-line who might have been racist or bullies. They were big and I saw it as my job to teach them a lesson every chance we got in practice. The best feeling was not to yell at the person or get into a fight with them, but to take away their pride. Every day their coach would yell at them to stop me, but they couldn't. They had to go and apologize to their quarterback for allowing me to hit them.

Football can also be a petty place, full of ego and attitudes. There was a time during practice; we were doing a seven-on-seven drill. The rushing linebacker would come in, try to make a move on the running back, and then everyone would ease off. It was a drill to allow the quarterback to feel the pressure of someone coming at him. It was not a drill for anyone to get hurt or do full contact. I happened to be fast enough to put moves on guys and, for the most part, the running backs could not stop me. I was getting to the quarterback and then letting up. The coach was getting so angry that he told the running back to cut my legs. Think about it, we are on the same team in a drill, learning technique but going hard. It was understood by all. No hitting below the waist and only one move against each other and stop. That was it. The coach told a walk-on, who loved the game of football and was so happy to be there, to cut my legs from under me. Don was there and heard the whole thing. He couldn't believe his ears. We were on the same team. We were all supposed to be a teammate. I was prepared for anything but not to that extent, so I leaned forward, knowing I was going to beat the person assigned to block me. I could beat him pretty easily, and I wasn't going to try to kill him, just do our standard moves and go on to the next play. The ball snapped and I went full speed to the point of contact and then eased up. In the blink of an eye, he dives at my knees. I'm down, crawling on the ground.

I was pissed. I was angry. The running back was waving his hand in the air, screaming that he was sorry. He was scared. I was the star recruit, and I was down. He was only doing what he was told, but I was crawling toward him like the terminator. I was screaming that I was going to kill him, and nothing was going to stop me. If I got my hands on him, I would not stop until his body was limp in my hands. The kid was scared. Not only did he hurt the star recruit, but he was going to get murdered. Don ran up to me, "Ken, Ken, it wasn't his fault. He was told to cut you." I couldn't hear anything. I kept crawling toward my victim.

"Ken."

"I'm sorry," the kid yelled.

"Ken," Don yelled again.

I registered his voice, but I was hurt. I was like a wounded animal, ready to attack anything. My career could have been over and for what? A coach did not like the idea that I was beating his guys in practice. We were on the same team! The sad reality is that no one would have known what happened. My career could have been over, and football would have moved on. I could have gotten to that kid and done some damage to him. Both our careers would have been over, and that tag would have stuck with me all my football life. So many things could have happened, and the coach would not be blamed. Sometimes I get frustrated at what I see as an injustice to players when their careers are destroyed by coaches who never take the brunt of the blame.

I was able to overcome my injury and continue to play the season. I was a good player and while all the scouts were watching Hardy Nickerson, they saw me. Hardy was smart, fast, and could play. I marveled at how well he played the game and hoped that some of it would rub off on me. Hardy went in the fifth round and played sixteen years in the NFL. That's incredible since the average life of an NFL player is a little over four years. The position he played was middle linebacker. I know the scouts had to look at me a bit since they were there looking at him. I hoped to have a good year and to prove to some of the people in my past that I was not a failure. I wanted to make my parents proud and to represent Laney Junior College well. Where was God in all of this? He was there. Did I worship Him? Not as much; yet, regardless of what I did, God was faithful to His word.

So shall my word be that goes out from my mouth; it shall not return to me empty, but it shall accomplish that which I purpose, and shall succeed in the thing for which I sent it. "For you shall go out in joy and be led forth in peace; the mountains and the hills before you shall break forth into singing, and all the trees of the field shall clap their hands. Instead of the thorn shall come up the cypress; instead of the brier shall come up the myrtle; and it shall make a name for the Lord, an everlasting sign that shall not be cut off. (Isaiah 55:11-13 – ESV)

I was getting all that I prayed for, yet I started to believe it was me instead of God. As I did my interviews with my newly found fame, I would shyly try to mention God as my way of repayment to Him for saving me and directing my path. But God wants us to speak His name boldly, not just whisper and be afraid. I remember an interview where I said the reason I was here was that God got me here and the reporter said, "Yea, but you had a lot to do with it. It was your hard work and dedication that got you this far." It was true, to a point, but it would not have been without God guiding and pushing me to become who I was.

As the old saying goes, "Don't read your press clippings." I started to and started to push God in a corner and enjoy being Ken Harvey. There are things that I have done that I am not proud of, things that I could dismiss and chalk up to a college kid experience, but wrong is wrong and I was wrong a lot of times. There are a lot of things that I should probably apologize for. I could not judge anyone, lest I be judged myself.

I walked around campus with people whom everyone thought were strange to hang around. There was a girl who was mostly paralyzed and had some disabilities, but she was a student at Cal. I am not sure how she did it, but she was a student, and I was a friend. We would go to most places on campus and to study hall. It was a strange friendship to most, but, for me, it was seeing people beyond their physical bodies and looking into their souls.

I had money, or at least a scholarship, and during the season I could eat with the team. I had a good first year and had become somewhat of a star on the team. Don and I did our interviews, and people liked me. I may have been quiet, but

I was not stupid. My speech class from my junior college paid off because I knew what to say. Some of the classes were easy, some hard. I had to gain an understanding of the professors and learn to write papers that would appeal to their egos. I was getting by in the classroom, the same bad habits I had as a kid never worked their way out of my system.

There was one opportunity that I would get paid by a powerful alumnus who loved Cal players who would do some summer work when school was out. I hoped for that to be true, and it came true as I got a job working at his house. It was an older guy who lived in the hills of Oakland. I was smiling because I knew this was going to be the moment. The alumni and his wife had to be in their seventies and like a lion on the prowl, I had my mark. We shook hands and he introduced himself to me and the other guys that would work for him that day. He took us to the side of his house and gave us our job. He lived on the side of a large hill and the city told him that he had to clear all the grass, brush, and weeds from the hill for fire prevention. Where was the weed wacker? He informed us that we had to get a hoe and dig everything up by its roots. This was no small hill, but he was the alumni, and I was going to do my job well. I wanted to show them that I did not mind working, and to top it off, the alumni would stand at the top of the hill with his arms folded and just look at us. He had on overalls, the outdoor boots, and the straw hat and shades. I was sweating and hating life.

Lunchtime came around and I was starving. His wife said that she would make lunch for us and gave us lemonade from the trees that grew in her garden. That was a bonus because I did not bring any money or have any food, so anything free was perfect for me. Did I mention that they were in their seventies? The food was bad, and the lemonade was bitter. Her taste buds were gone, so she couldn't tell if it was sweet or sour. We ate and tried not to frown. After all, they were sweet and she felt that she was helping us, so who were we to complain. When we were alone, we all had a good laugh. When we finished up, I figured this was the moment I had been waiting for. I know it was against the rules for the college to give us money, but for alumni to give us a bit extra, I would be cool with that. The gentleman walked up to us after we worked for several hours. I intentionally worked the hardest doing the areas that others did not want to do. He gathered us around and said that he was going to pay us. "Let me see, how much are they paying nowadays?" he spoke. He was giving us minimum wages, and to add insult to injury, he said he was going to give 10 percent more. He paid us $5 an hour for eight hours of work; that's 45 dollars plus 10%. I busted my butt for $49.50. Now I wasn't being ungrateful. I got paid, but I was mad. I thought this was going to be the big score. I was going to be rolling with the big money. That was my life lesson.

"For the kingdom of heaven is like a landowner who went out early in the morning to hire workers for his vineyard. *He agreed to pay them a denarius for the day and sent them into his vineyard. "About nine in the morning, he went out and saw others standing in the marketplace doing nothing. He told them, 'You also go and work in my vineyard, and I will pay you whatever is right.' So, they went. "He went out again about noon and about three in the afternoon and did the same thing. About five in the afternoon, he went out and found still others standing around. He asked them, 'Why have you been standing here all day long doing nothing?' "'Because no one has hired us,' they answered. "He said to them, 'You also go and work in my vineyard.' "When evening came, the owner of the vineyard said to his foreman, 'Call the workers and pay them their wages, beginning with the last ones hired and going on to the first.' "The workers who were hired about five in the afternoon came and each received a denarius. So when those came who were hired first, they expected to receive more. But each one of them also received a denarius. When they received it, they began to grumble against the landowner. 'These who were hired last worked only one hour,' they said, 'and you have made them equal to us who have borne the burden of the work and the heat of the day.' "But he answered one of them, 'I am not being unfair to you, friend. Didn't you agree to work for a denarius? Take your pay and go. I want to give the one who was hired last the same as I gave you. Don't I have the right to do what I want with my own money? Or are you envious because I am generous?' "So, the last will be first, and the first will be last."* (St. Matthew 20:1-16)

9

Superhero

I believe in people and believe that we should treat each other with respect, so when issues arise, I try to help in the best I can. I always rationalize: what if that was one of my parents or brothers, sisters or wife that needed help, wouldn't I want someone to help them? That was what the Bible taught and something I truly believed. In Oakland, while in school at Laney Junior College, before I made it to the University of California, there was a man who was drunk or on drugs when he started to get on a bus. He stopped on the first step and looked around. He decided that would be his new spot and he would not move. The bus driver was a woman, and you could tell that the stress of driving a bus was taking its toll on her. There were female bus drivers who had been raped, robbed, and beaten up in the past and so stress was always present. If they are pretty, they get hit on. If they are not strong or don't know how to handle themselves, they were like small prey in a field of lions. She appeared to be at the end of her wits and was not going to take any more crap from anyone. He picked the wrong day to mess with her. My then-girlfriend Janice and I were sitting upfront, so we have a full preview of everything that took place. She told him, "Sir, please pay your fare." He looked at her dumbfounded and said nothing. She sighed, "Sir, please either pay your money and get in or leave. You can't just block the door." He swayed from the alcohol and continued to look at her. "Sir, I have to get going. Please get in or get out." He was not going to move. Janice and I watched and said nothing. This was not my battle. The bus driver got up from her seat and moved toward him. "I'm so tired of this shit," she said. *This can't be good,* we thought. She tried to move him, but he would not budge. I believe the bus drivers had to make their routes by a certain time and keep on schedule or they would get fined. She was getting really upset. She moved toward him and in a flurry of punches, hit him in the face and body. We sat there with our mouths wide open. This was not something you see every day, and this was way before cell phones. People on the bus were pointing and laughing, but no action. No one did anything, except the superhero, me. What if that was my mother or sister? I had to do something. I jumped up and stood between her and the guy. His face was bloodied, and he was still swaying but I'm sure he felt nothing. "Miss," I said putting my body between them, "It is not worth it. He is not worth you losing your job. I'll get him off." I turned to the man. "Sir, please just leave." The guy held on not moving, yet still swaying. The bus driver was over the top. Everything bottled up was coming out. I looked at Janice to make sure I was doing the right thing. Janice's eyes became wide as she pointed toward my midsection. It was a subtle point, but one that I could read. I looked down to where she was pointing. The bus driver had pulled out a huge blade and I was the only one standing between her and the drunk. One of my neighbors growing up had been murdered because he tried to break up a fight between a husband and wife. He was stabbed to death by the husband for trying to be a good guy. He didn't even know them but was trying to do the right thing. I was on the brink of doing the same thing. I politely excused myself and sat back down. My involvement was over. Thank God the guy got off the bus. The bus driver was in tears. She was at her last straw. Janice and I prayed the rest of the way home.

On another occasion, Janice and I were walking home. Although Janice did not go to Cal, she lived nearby. We were walking and talking when we heard a scream. Superhero Ken to the rescue again. There were places in Oakland where the law of the land was not to get involved, but I couldn't just do anything. I had watched too many good TV shows, seen my parents try to help people, and seen too many people do nothing. I heard the scream and was ready for action. I saw a guy running like his hair was on fire. The scream came again: "Stop him, please stop him." For a second, I thought about letting it go. This was not my business. Since he was running, and she was screaming, I assumed she wasn't hurt, but I still could not let it go. I had to do something. I ran after the guy. It was stupid. I left Janice standing there alone and went after him, but it seemed like the right thing to do. I got near to him but kept enough distance to make sure I knew what I was doing before I attacked. He stopped and turned. He put his hand in his coat pocket and moved toward me. He said, "Take one more step and I will blow your fucking head off." You could probably smell the rubber from my tennis shoes as I hit the brakes. I wasn't trying to die. I started to do some *Star Trek* Captain Kirk type of stuff. I dodged in and out, tucked and rolled. I looked for something to hide behind. He was scared. After shouting a bit more he threw her purse to the ground and took off. I picked up the purse and saw Janice and the lady coming toward me. Janice was scared for me. Fear and anger are close brothers, and so she was also mad that I had done something so stupid. I handed the lady the purse and she sighed, "Thank God he didn't take any of my credit cards." My life and her screams for help were all for credit cards that could have been replaced. The big fat "S" on my chest was not for

Superman, but Stupid man. A stupid man saved the day again.

Another example: I was walking home from school late in the evening; I was still living in the dorms at the time. Berkeley is in the hills, so some areas are surrounded by trees and were not always lit at night. It didn't matter. I hardly thought anyone was going to jump out and attack me. I was walking alone until I heard a scream and then saw some commotion. I cautiously moved toward the sound and found a man and a woman fighting with each other. Her top was ripped. I didn't see how it got ripped, but they seemed to be a couple who just broke up and he was demanding his ring back. She did not want to give it back. I paused; I had to do something. I couldn't walk by and do nothing, that would be wrong. I walked up and separated them. I suggested that each of them should go their own way and that it was not worth someone going to jail or getting hurt over. She said she wanted to go. The man grabbed her and said that she was not going anywhere without giving up the ring. I looked at her. "Miss, just give him the ring and then get home safely." She said that she was not giving up anything. I sighed. I knew this was going nowhere fast. I couldn't foresee a peaceful conclusion.

A sound pushed through the darkness of the night and a skinny white kid appeared on a moped ready to assess the situation. Maybe he read the same books I did or watched the same shows; either way, he was going to help. What he saw were two Black guys and a Black woman with her shirt ripped and crying. I imagine a thousand things must have been going through his head. He asked the lady if everything was alright. The lady replied that she just wanted to go home. Once again the other guy says she was not going anywhere without giving him back his ring. It was the same dance I witnessed before, yet now I was an actor in the movie. The kid on the bike told the lady to hop on. I look in amazement knowing this was not going to be good. The woman got on the bike, and I stood there watching and wondering what the kid is thinking. He was going to get us all killed. Life can change in seconds; it was his turn to be a superhero and to save the day. This was a moment he had practiced mentally all his life. He went into his pocket and pulled out a can of mace. Inexperience and fear got the better of him. He jerked the can so hard it flew out of his hands. The can of the mace rolled by my feet. My only thought was this kid is going to get us both killed. I shook my head in disgust at his attempt. The man started to move toward him, "I'm going to get my ring." He was smaller than me but bigger than the kid on the bike. It may have been his ring and maybe she should give it back. I was in the process of trying to figure things out before our little hero on the bike showed up. Now, this might have been stupidity on my part, but I reached down and picked up the mace and handed it to the kid. I shook my head as if to say, "Kid, if you are going to pull it out, you better be prepared for whatever happens." The kid took the mace and sprayed it in the guy's face. I stood there dumbfounded. Maybe it was me that should have been prepared. What in the world just happened? The guy was screaming, "I am going to kill someone," as his face was on fire because of the mace. He rubbed his burning eyes and swung wildly. The woman got on the bike and they took off. Now it was just me and a mad man screaming that he is going to kill someone. I weighed my options and started to walk in the other direction. I decided I didn't need to be a hero that day.

One last superhero story to share. Maybe I put myself in positions for them to happen or maybe God put me there to help, who knows? Don, my best friend from college, and I were driving in his car when we saw this old white lady in a wheelchair with groceries struggling to make it across the street. I looked at her and had a thought that we should help her. Don told me that it was not a good idea. I tried to convince him that it was. This is the Bible in action. Help the elderly. That's what we are supposed to do. She was struggling to get across and she was at a blind spot to any speeding car that might be coming up the hill. I couldn't let it go. We had to do something. I convinced Don to turn around and go back. He pulled up next to her and I rolled down my window: "Ma'am, can I help you?" Her face turned pale white and her eyes widened. The woman screamed, dropped her groceries, and began to franticly push her wheelchair. We sped away. Don looked at me and I bowed my head and accepted that he was right. I concluded that you cannot help everyone and not everyone wants to be helped. That could have gone wrong in so many ways.

Sometimes you can become a hero for no reason other than just stepping out and doing what others have not done. I once spent the night on the streets in San Francisco. It was not a big deal. I had missed my train and figured that it would be interesting to experience what it would be like to be homeless. It was a scary experience, trying to find a place to sleep, knowing that no matter how big you were, once you dozed off all your defenses were gone and at any moment someone could take your life. But once the word of my experiment got to the school newspapers at Cal, I became a hero to those who would never think of the homeless. I became a small voice for those who are invisible on the streets. Sometimes the platform you have allows your light to shine brighter. "*No one lights a lamp and puts it in a place where it will be hidden, or under a bowl. Instead, they put it on its stand, so that those who come in may see the light.*" (Luke 11:33).

10

The Turning Point

During my second year at Cal, we got a new coach. Joe Kapp had a losing year, and he had a reputation as a wild guy, which made me wonder what the heck I had stepped into. There was a rumor he pulled out his pecker during an interview and said, "If you want to write about something, I will give you something to write about," and proceeded to unzip his pants. The following year there was a new coach, and his name was Bruce Snyder. It was a good move for the school. Snyder had a good game plan and wanted to win. My fame was growing, and I made several of the covers for the school magazines. I had been hurt a few times during my career at Cal, which were some of the same injuries I had faced at Laney. My ankles or knees would hold me back and like the reality of so many football players, no matter how great you are, an injury can stop you in your tracks. There was a time I hyper-extended my knee and could barely walk. I thought there was no way I was going to play in the game we had coming up. I couldn't walk without my knee going backward and then being in excruciating pain. I still had the mindset never to quit, and I did train my mind to ignore a certain amount of pain, but this was beyond me. I couldn't even walk to class. The team gave me a knee brace to walk around the campus that week. It was still painful, but I was able to move. I made up my mind that there was no way I was going to play. Even with the brace, I could barely move.

I was limping through campus one day, and a guy came up to me out of nowhere. I assumed he was a fan and tried to be as polite as possible, but he went on to talk about his walk with the Lord and what God was doing in his life. He asked if I knew Jesus Christ, and I nodded yes. It was not a lie. I knew Jesus, but it was kind of like asking if I knew former President Obama. Yes, I know him. I've seen him on TV, met him twice in person, and read all about him, but I didn't have a personal relationship with him. The guy looks at me and asked if he could pray for my knee. I thought, "Come on, dude, you want to pray for my knee? I don't know you. We just met on the street, and you want to pray for my knee?" This was another Christian weirdo. I thought maybe if I said yes, he would stop talking to me and I could go on my merry way. He told me he would lay hands on my knees and pray. I'm thinking he is not just a weirdo, but he wants to draw attention to us so that I could somehow now be a part of his cult. I was still quiet, still cared about what people thought of me, but I did want to play in the game and so I thought the potential good could out weigh the bad and so I said, "Go ahead." He bent over and began to pray for my knee. I don't know if people stopped to look, I just wanted this to be over with as quickly as possible. He was praying aloud. He prayed for my knee, and believe it or not, it felt better, maybe because I wanted to get rid of him, but I did feel something. I had always been wary of preachers who laid hands on people and then take their money. I thought church was a show and a lot of what they did was hypocritical, but at the same time, I was walking in the reality of what the church had done for me. I might have been the hypocrite. I was walking in unbelief based on what I thought but living in the proof. I went on to play in the game I thought I would never be able to play in. I led the team in tackles and my knee held up. The win and pats on the back overshadowed what God did for me that day. It brought to my mind the Israelites, who cried out for food and God blessed them with it, and then they forgot as soon as they had another problem.

In my senior year, we had a chance to do something most teams never experienced. We traveled to Japan to play in

what was called the Coca-Cola Bowl. It was something
scheduled for teams to show football to other countries. This
was my first time out of the country, and I was excited. I was
one of the stars of the team and we were going to play
Washington State in Japan. This was a big deal for me and
everyone else. This was 1987 and teams did not travel overseas
that much. We discovered some sad truths there. Other
countries based their beliefs on what they saw in America. For
example, on a bus tour, most of the guys on the bus were Black.
We were sitting there riding to go somewhere. I remember
seeing billboards with the face of a Black cartoon, "Blackie
Toothpaste," or something like that. The characters had dark
Black skin, large white eyes, and big red lips. We passed by the
signs and looked on in disbelief. Some guys were accustomed
to it, some had never seen anything like that before, but for the
people in Japan, it was normal. We had a small Asian tour guide
who was happily showing us around. She was so full of energy
and wanting to be a good guide, she went on to tell us a story
to occupy our time. She decided to tell us the story of how
God made man. I remember us looking at each other thinking
this could not be going anywhere good, but we were going to
give it a try. She jovially began.

     She said, "God made the earth and saw that it was
good. He was excited to put the animals on it and everything
else as a part of the earth. Next, He was going to make man,

His greatest creation, so God took some of the clay and put it in the oven to bake. He was so excited by His creation that He took it out too early and thus it was undercooked and so the white man was created." She was getting more excited as she was telling this story. We looked at each other hoping, praying this story was not going in the direction that we thought it was. She began to talk about how God took the same dough and said this time He was not going to pull it out too early. He would wait. He waited so long that He overcooked His creation and that is how He created the Black man, and because the pan was so hot, they could dance well. Nice freaking touch. We all sat there with our mouths and eyes wide open. We probably looked like the pictures that we saw driving by. I was thinking, "Please shut up or there may be a riot on this bus." I'm sure she saw the looks on our faces, and hastily finished the story. She obviously did not get the same reactions as she did with the normal white tourist. "The third time, God was going to get it right," she said, "So He kept it in just the right amount of time, but He ran out of dough and that is why the Japanese people are so short." We all just rode in silence the rest of the way.

I did get a chance to be interviewed by an Asian reporter. Overall, everyone was sweet, even the lady who told us the story. It was nothing malicious, but something they had been given from the west. I was told through a translator that

I would be interviewed. A tiny female reporter would be talking, and I was to come around the corner and lift her up in my arms. I could do that. She began speaking and I was given my cue. I came around the corner, and it sounded like an old Godzilla movie. She was talking in her language and then I came around the corner and lifted her up. I could have sworn I heard her call me Godzilla, but I couldn't be sure. I picked her up expecting her to weigh as much as an American woman, and nearly threw her in the air. She was like a child, weighing no more than 90 pounds. The game in Japan ended in a tie. We traveled all that distance to end a game in a tie with a score of 17 to 17. I was voted the most valuable defensive player of the game. I found some old footage of the game on the internet. I wasn't that good. I hustled a lot and made some big plays, but my technique was bad. I did not shed blockers as well as I should have. Thank God I was strong enough to cause some problems at the point of attack and I had good teammates that forced the quarterback to hold the ball longer than he should have. Looking back made me realize that when you think you are all that, you forget that it was a team that got you there.

There were two post-season games that I chose to attend. I wanted to play in the East-West Shrine Game and the Senior Bowl. There were two very simple reasons. The East-West Shrine game was close to home and coaches from both Laney and Cal could come to see one of their own play the game. I could also have my friends and my girlfriend Janice come to watch me play. The second reason was that the Senior Bowl players received payment, so this would be the first time I would get paid. The East-West Shrine Game was important, based on a lot of factors. As I reread old clippings, the biggest thing that stood out was no one knew that much about me. There were a lot of big-name players that played in that game. It was by the grace of God that I was allowed to participate in any post-season game, but I was there, and I was going to make the best of it. I was still an unknown to those outside the football world, and to a lot of people in it, but I was there to show my stuff. Some top players already attracted a lot of media attention, so it was easy to get lost in the press. There were guys like Don McPherson, Gordie Lockbaum, Lorenzo White, Sterling Sharpe, Chad Hennings (Outland Winner), and Paul McGowan (Butkus Winner). These were big names at the time.

It is very difficult to become a star or even make it to the NFL. Almost every player in the NFL was a star in their school. In my mind, I was not about to be washed away into nothingness. This was my chance to show off in front of everyone who knew me in the Bay area. In my first game of the East-West Shrine, I ended the game with ten tackles, one sack, one pass deflection, and a critical three-down play, stopping their star player one yard short of making the first down. People were starting to take notice and I was starting to shine. I was voted the most valuable defensive player of the game. I should have given the credit to my girlfriend Janice. On the day of the game, we got into an argument. It was comical, or at least it was on my part, and maybe that released most of my stress and allowed me to just play. I'm not sure what we were arguing about, but we were getting into it. I remember picking Janice up and holding her in my arms. I remember her screaming for me to put her down. I was the obedient boyfriend, so I dropped her on the floor. She was ready to kick my butt. In the end, we had a good laugh, but I won't be doing that ever again.

The last game I played was the Senior Bowl. It was going to be the first game that I could get paid and send some money back to my parents. The game was played in Mobile Ala, down south. How do you stand out? Make big plays in big games. I had quarterback sacks in the Senior Bowl and it started to get me noticed. I was voted the outstanding defensive player of that game as well. A lot of people said they had never heard of me. Now they had. I was on the fast track to getting drafted, something I had not thought about much. I wanted to just give it my all, and never give up. In a way, I was fighting the demons that I had from my youth and would not stop until I won. I would not be a quitter. In a time before all the media-rich TV, cable, and the internet, I was invited to go to the NFL combines. We were given numbers and ushered to different events that would test our skills against each other. This was where you got a chance to see that no matter how good you were, there were always those who were better. To be honest, the reason you make it so far is you must have a bit of cockiness in you, and I was no different. I knew I was strong, and I wanted to show everyone there how strong and fast I was.

I remember taking a physical and doing the normal testing, including the weigh-in. We had to walk down the middle of a pathway where scouts sat on both sides of the aisle. Each player had to walk the "green mile" to the scale when called. As you took the walk, you could hear the scouts talking to each other, and taking notes. You walk up to the scale and they announce your name, number, and what school you were from. You would take off your shirt and get on the scale and they would call out the number. I was muscular, so I expected them to be a bit shocked. I had six perecent body fat without trying to diet. I had a 33" waist and looked more like a bodybuilder than a football player. There was nothing funnier than seeing old scouts take their glasses off to get a better look at you or for a group of people to collectively stop talking and look. It was like the "E.F. Harvey" thing all over again. This was a nickname Joe Kapp gave me, which was a play off the old E.F Hutton commercial. There was this commercial with various people sitting around talking or doing something, and then when someone mentioned that they used E.F Hutton to do their stocks and everyone would stop what they were doing and listen to what his advice was. Everyone was looking at me and I liked it.

There was a guy named Vincent Brown who came into the room as a potential draft pick. He was a quiet guy, who also played linebacker. His nickname was "The Undertaker," and it was given to him long before the WWE wrestler. He took the long walk, and when he took off his shirt, there was a collective gasp. The scouts began writing furiously. Have you ever stood next to someone, and because they are so superior, you wish you could shrink and disappear into nothingness? That was how I felt when he took his shirt off. I no longer felt I had the best body, and I was no longer as cocky after that.

I ruled the bench press. The goal was to see how many times you could bench press 225 pounds. I knew I was going to kill it because I was strong. I had the strength of most linemen and the body of a linebacker. I bench press 225 pounds thirty-two times. It was cool and there was nothing like having people cheer you on. The feeling of strangers wanting you to do more, pushing you to do more. I pushed with all I had and kicked some butt. That year I broke their record for the standing long jump and had a 38" vertical jump. I was killing it. I had a fast shuttle time and then came the time for the forty-yard dash, where they measure how fast you can run downfield. There had been horror stories of guys who went down in the draft because of this. I was scared. I had a pair of running shoes that were not designed for speed, but good enough to get the job done. There were people here frantically trying to get an advantage. Ken Norton Jr was there, and he was a beast. He was one of those guys you knew by reputation. His father was a famous boxer. He had good track shoes, and he just happened to be my size. A small act of kindness can mean the world to someone else. It was a good lesson to learn, and one that has served me well. Ken Norton allowed me to borrow his track shoes to run my forty. He didn't have to do that, we were all competing for a job in the NFL, and we were all linebackers. It was something that helped me immensely. In a game where seconds count, I was able to decrease my forty-yard time to 4.52. I think it was the second-fastest time by any linebacker in that draft class. I felt like I had a great chance to make it to the pros. I was now proven and no longer a secret. I knew people started to talk.

I had taken a trip to New York once to speak with Bill Parcell about the draft, to see if they were interested in me. We had a conversation; he looked me over and, clasping his hands together, leaned forward as if to show he was going to be straight with me. He looked at me and said that while I was impressive, he saw me as more of a third-down cover guy who could come in and cover backs out of the backfield. I was too small to be one of his full timeline backers. They were all over 260 and he did not see that for me. I smiled and was polite, but in my mind, I was burning. A few ungodly words under my breath and I vowed that I was going to show him. It would be a mistake not drafting me. The Giants were scratched off the list of teams I wanted to play for, but in the NFL draft, you don't have a choice. I had no choice, but I still knew where I did not want to go.

On draft day, my mom flew up to be with me. I think my dad stayed home with my other brothers and sister. I don't think they could afford to buy two plane tickets. Joe Martin was now my agent. It was a four-year wait for him, but it paid off. I had the potential to go high in the draft, which would be good for all. This was an era before the draft was televised, so I had my draft party at Charles Gatson's grandmother's home. He was my friend from Laney, and even though we did not go to the same four-year college, we still shared a bond that was forged by our struggles to get out of junior college. I tried to keep it low-key. I had heard stories of other players who had put a lot of money into draft parties only to see themselves go a lot further down than they thought. I didn't want to suffer that same type of embarrassment. Janice was there by my side and the good news is, she later became my wife. In the 1988 draft, everyone was looking for pass rushers like Lawrence

Taylor, LT. Everyone wanted players to play like him, but like superman in the comics there were several duplicates, but nothing like the original. I was a clone of that pass rusher. The first pick in the draft was Aundray Bruce by the Atlanta Falcons. It was good and bad news. Because he was the first pick, it was a great indication that passes rushers were what everyone was looking for and that happened to be what I was. The bad news was that because he was a linebacker, he was not going to get paid as much as a quarterback. His numbers would set the bar. I sat around watching everyone ahead of me get picked. I did have some press at Charles's house, but it was nothing big. I don't think a lot of people thought I would get taken in the first round. Suddenly the phone rang, and we all watched it. It was after the eleventh pick, so I was excited. I get a phone call from Larry Wilson, the general manager of the Cardinals. He asked me if I wanted to be a Cardinal. I said, "Heck yeah." He told me to hold. We all sat around and watch on TV as the team picked me as their twelfth pick. I was a Cardinal. The team had just moved from St. Louis to Phoenix, so I became the original Phoenix Cardinal. Most people said, Ken who? Now that I was picked, it was my job to prove to them that they got a bargain. *And God is able to bless you abundantly, so that in all things at all times, having all that you need, you will abound in every good work.* (2 Corinthians 9:8).

11

God Saves Me Because He Loves Me

Don and I were at a boxing match I had agreed to do security for before I got drafted. I had to keep my word even though I no longer needed the job. The match was between an Irish and Mexican boxer. The room was divided with fans of one group on one side and fans of the other fighter on the other side. They were kind enough to introduce me as Ken Harvey, the guy who just got drafted to the Phoenix Cardinals. Everyone in the audience looked like they either didn't care or were confused. They might have heard of the St Louis Cardinals but who in the heck were the Phoenix Cardinals? They were there for a boxing match, and they couldn't care less about a player they had never heard of playing for a team they could care less about. I walked into the ring, and just like a

Rocky movie, I raised my hands and went around tapping the boxers' gloves. They looked at their gloves, then at me with a blank expression. I moved on and didn't care. I was a star living the dream except there were no cheers, no applause, but I was still drafted, and no one could take that away from me. The fight went on and the winner was announced. We could tell that there might be trouble. Both sides did not like each other, and throughout the fight, there were small squabbles. It was beyond people just getting mad because of what they thought were bad calls from the referee. It had become a racial divide combined with lots of drinks to add fuel to the fire. The announcement was made and like a match being lit, the start of several big fights broke out. The fights continued until the whole room was fighting. It was one side against the other. One race against the other. It was getting real. I looked at Don. He said to stay where we were and let the police handle it. They were not paying us enough to get into the mix. I couldn't just stand by and watch, someone might get hurt, and we were security. I ran into the middle of the battle. Don reluctantly followed behind me because that's what friends do. In his words, "it looked like the Red Sea closing behind us" as we traveled into the mix. We were dead smack in the middle of it all and there was no one else around to help us. I began pulling people apart. There were a lot of fights, and it was stupid thinking I could help, but I was pumped up and high on the excitement of helping someone. I was also cocky because I just got drafted. I was a walking superhero.

Everything that I saw on TV or read in a comic book was coming true. I had just broken up a fight when I felt a shove. It was a powerful shove that nearly knocked me down. I got my balance and turned to see a large white guy. He must have been about 6'6", weighing 280 pounds. He looked as though he was going to fight me. I reverted to what I had been seeing all my life. I broke down into a karate stance and yelled at him that I would kill him if he ever touched me again. I would take his heart out of his body and throw it to the ground and step on it. I was a crouching tiger, hidden Negro. Don watched in amazement. He paused, puzzled that I never told him I knew karate. He waited because he was now going to see a show and wanted to be around to tell the tale. The only problem was, I never took karate. I had never really fought before in my life. It was all an act, but it worked. The big guy extended his hands as if to say please don't hit me. "I am a big fan," he said and walked away. My back leg was shaking so bad; I nearly fell over. Don ran up to congratulate me. I did what you should never do in a fight: I stopped to congratulate myself while still amid the battle. The next thing I knew, I was on my butt. Someone was thrown into the back of my legs. I went down.

I was now a prime candidate to get taken out. Don

came to my rescue and pulled me up so fast I barely had time to think. Things were getting out of hand. Someone had just gotten stabbed in another location that I had just been to. All this was happening right after I got drafted. I was going to die before I ever made it to the NFL. We both saw the San Francisco Riot Squad come in. It was something straight out of a movie. It was cool. I watched as they had their riot squad uniforms and shields. They marched down and broke everything up. My career was saved. Sometimes angels fight our battles without us even knowing it. *"Know therefore that the Lord your God is God; he is the faithful God, keeping his covenant of love to a thousand generations of those who love him and keep his commandments."* (Deuteronomy 7:9).

I am Ken Harvey. Drafted twelfth pick in the first round of the NFL.

Epilogue

If this book was a game, it would be my pre-game: the things you do leading up to the game, the experiences you practice every day to get you to the point of walking out on the big field. I would love to say everything worked out perfectly, but, like a football game, there are some good plays and some bad plays, some touchdowns, and some fumbles. The goal at the end of every game is to win; not just to play the game and be content to get on the field but to win the game. My story is not over, but this is the start. It has taken a long time for me to write this book. A lot of people told me to write it a long time ago, but I hesitated because I did not think anyone would want to hear my story. I had very low self-esteem. God's will must be done, regardless of what we think. It may not happen when it should, but at the end of the day, His timing is right.

I'm a work in progress. I write to show you what God can do, and how His blessings can flow. As I searched through a multitude of self-help books, I realized a very simple truth; most of the principles are the same. We must believe in something, which acts as our GPS to guide us to where our destination might be. You must act. You may have to take several detours along the way, but that is okay. In the end, we win and get to our destination.

Fear is in opposition to faith. Fear stops a lot of good people from being great. It stops a lot of people from acting. God will nudge, He will suggest, but He will not force. It doesn't matter who you are, how old you are, or whatever your situation is, God does not look at that. He sees you and how He wants to help you. It is never too late to change.

Your past helped you get here, but it does not dictate who you are. You can be born again. We all have gifts, and it is up to us to maximize our gifts. Whatever that gift is, God gave it to you, for you, but also for others. There are so many people who sit on their gifts and do nothing with them. The greatest lie from the enemy is to make you feel that what you have is not worth anything. You will have to do some work. Imagine someone giving you the material for a home, the land, and all the tools needed to build for free, but you still must build, or else you have nothing. I write this book for the young and the old. No matter where you are, it is okay. Consider this your starting point. The devil wants us to look at our lives and not believe the potential we have.

Young men and women, you can become whatever you want to be. That is the goal to strive for. You may go off track, but that is okay. At least you are moving.

I write this book for people who might be in that second stage of their lives. As football players, we often retire from a sport we've been playing all our lives, and then it is over. No going back to it. That is no different from a person getting ready to retire at 65, who starts wondering what else they can do; or maybe that 40-year-old who realizes they hate their job they have but are too afraid to make a change. Sometimes, changes are the best options; you must step out in faith. It's never too late, and you are never too old. Reject the lies the enemy has told you. You are better than that. I was a high school dropout. I was told that I was a loser and would be a loser all my life. I had to shift my thinking from what people thought about me and start living like whom God said I was. I want you to know that there's nothing God can't do. I am that I said I am. Remember what the Bible says in 1 Corinthians 9:24-27: *Do you not know that in a race all the runners run, but only one gets the prize? Run in such a way as to get the prize. Everyone who competes in the games goes into strict training. They do it to get a crown that will not last, but we do it to get a crown that will last forever. Therefore, I do not run like someone running aimlessly; I do not fight like a boxer beating the air. No, I strike a blow to my body and make it my slave so that after I have preached to others, I myself will not be disqualified for the prize.*

What am I saying? God counts you in when life counts you out. Don't let negative thoughts or people prevent you from living your full potential. There will always be those who try to tear you down: "You're not qualified." "You stutter." "You've made too many mistakes." "You're too short." "You're not that talented." All that is blatant lies just to make you feel discounted so you won't be able to actualize your dreams. Don't believe that. Don't fall into that trap because God has called us out into His marvelous light. What you have is about to be multiplied by God. He'll take you from the back to the front, from scarcity to abundance, from insignificance to great strength. You've been counted, you've been qualified, and what God said about your life will come true, and those aren't just nice, kind, encouraging words; they're a prophecy. If you accept it and say, "Yes, this is for me," you'll start to see it happen. God will amaze you with His goodness. God Bless.

ABOUT THE AUTHOR

Ken Harvey grew up in Austin, Texas. Shortly after attending U. C. Berkeley, he was selected for the first round, 12th overall, of the 1988 NFL draft by the Arizona Cardinals. There he played six seasons until signing with the Washington Football Team in 1994. He was selected to his fourth straight NFL Pro Bowl in 1997 and ended his career with 89 sacks, averaging 8.6 per season. Ken retired just prior to the start of the 1999 season. In 2002, Ken received the prestigious honor of being nominated in the Washington's highest accolade of "80 Greatest Redskins." Shortly after receiving that honor, he was chosen and inducted into the Redskins Ring of Fame at Fed Ex Field. He was nominated five consecutive times for the NFL Hall of Fame. His speaking portfolio includes sharing his insights and volunteering his time and talents to support many organizations. Ken is an author of several books and screenplays. He is currently co-authoring a children's book with American actor, artist, and former American football player, Terry Crews. Ken is currently a Marketing Associate for Fellows Financial group.

Made in the USA
Middletown, DE
25 October 2022

13407319R00083